Writing Your Way

Manjusvara

Windhorse Publications

Published by Windhorse Publications Ltd
169 Mill Road
Cambridge CB1 3AN
UK
email: info@windhorsepublications.com
web: www.windhorsepublications.com

First published 2005, reprinted in 2010 with minor corrections.

Cover Image John Foxx
Cover design Marlene Eltschig
Printed by Bell & Bain, Glasgow.

British Library Cataloguing in Publication Data:
A catalogue record for this book is available from the British Library.

ISBN: 978 1 899579 67 9

Chapter 14 first appeared in a slightly different form in *Dharma Life 21*,
and Chapter 28 first appeared in *Writing the Bright Moment*, Roselle Angwin, Fire in the Head, 2004.

Poem on p.98 from *Seeing Things* by Seamus Heaney, © 1991, Faber.

Contents

About the Author

Manjusvara was born David Keefe, in Hertfordshire, England in 1953. After studing composition at the Royal Northern College of Music in Manchester and research in electronic music at the University of Durham, he went on to write music for films, dance, and the theatre. In 1987 he was ordained within the Western Buddhist Order and given the name Manjusvara, which means 'gentle music'. For a number of years he worked for the Buddhist charity Karuna Trust, becoming Director of Fund-raising and Newsletter Editor. More recently he has divided his time between writing, editing, and teaching. His poems and essays have appeared in leading journals in England and America, and he is the editor for Weatherlight Press. He is a co-leader of 'Wolf at the Door' writing workshops and teaches regularly throughout the world.

Foreword

The single word that repeatedly returned to my mind while reading this book was 'compassion'. By this I don't mean compassion for those poor devils who are not writers, but for the whole of life (whatever that may be). David Keefe – or Manjusvara, as I know him – holds dear to his heart above all else William Blake's philosophy that 'Everything that lives is Holy.' That spirit pervades the book, and makes it far more than a text about how to write, or even about writing as a tool for change (though it is that also).

Wolf at the Door writing workshops, which Manjusvara and I teach together, emerged from an extremely tentative (at least in my mind) idea that writing might be much more than the production of a competent, publishable poem, story, play, or novel. Yet a clear image of exactly *what* it could be has revealed itself only gradually, mostly through watching our students discover hidden dimensions of themselves in the course of these workshops. In articulating this I have been aware that we are implicitly questioning many assumptions of our society at large: that 'art' is irrelevant to the health of society, that it 'makes nothing happen', that art and religion are separate entities that have nothing to say to each other, that 'creative writing' is something you do when you have failed to make it in the world, that 'creativity' and 'fantasy' are synonymous.

The thinking behind Wolf at the Door springs from the age-old idea that the human imagination contains a kind of wisdom, a vision of wholeness, which we ignore at our peril. Indeed, in these impoverished times when the indwelling wisdom of imagination is needed as never before, the concept of art as an integrating force, an entrance into the spiritual, and a path (rather than a distraction or entertainment) which anyone can tread, while not new, is pre-eminently valuable, even essential, to the process of becoming whole – wholly human – that is implicit in the Buddhist philosophy on which our workshops are based.

Manjusvara is a man not merely of great talent (among other things he is a charity fund-raiser, publisher, writing tutor, and accomplished poet), but of insight and humanity. He's a man who fully lives his philosophy, whose daily life is an enactment of his core beliefs. That is why this book will be of great interest to all those who are trying to live emotionally richer and more harmonious lives in a world dogged by materialism and pressure to conform.

While providing expert guidance through a number of writing exercises, Manjusvara also manages to achieve something I've not found in any other book about writing: the communication of the secret life that all serious writers of necessity create out of their efforts to explore their complex and often challenging relationship with the world. As such, the book is an invitation to share in that life and to commit oneself to a path which, although it may begin in familiar territory, will sooner or later lead us into regions that may change us deeply – even magnificently – and for ever.

Ananda

Bristol
5 May 2004

For Sarvamitra who gave me
the idea, and Ananda who
gave me many of the ideas.

And for my mother, my late father,
and my brother for all their
encouragement and support.

1

The Swept Room

You don't have to be inspired to write, but you do need a way: a means to express things which are uniquely yours. This book lays out such a path: a series of exercises that you can apply to your own preoccupations and your own circumstances; a means to take you deeper into your experiences and, as a consequence, take them more seriously. It is about learning how to unlock your creativity, how to let language work through you and begin dancing across the page. I have written it because it is my passionate belief that there is not one of us who does not have a creative spark in us somewhere. We all have things to say, but we need constructive encouragement to help us to say them. The secret lies in learning to trust ourselves. Teaching writing workshops around the world has convinced me that this trust is something that can be learned: that through consistent effort we can become free from the limiting habits and views that undervalue so much of what we do. It is a search for the wholeness which, from the Buddhist perspective I will be taking, should be the goal of any vibrant spiritual practice.

If you doubt this capacity for self-expression, then consider that virtually everything we do is easily recognizable as being our own – the way we walk down a street, the way we write our signature, the way we pick up the telephone. For example, there is in Buddhism a teaching which intimates that you can learn a lot about someone from the way they go about sweeping a room. Do they do it in a wild fashion, dust flying everywhere? Or do they go about it more calmly and methodically? Sweeping a room may seem far removed from what is usually thought of as the spiritual life, but it is shrewd to make this connection. Every act is built upon all that has gone before, and even the way we approach a simple task is likely to reflect our deepest most subjective patterns, all the hopes and fears that go to make us what we are.

Writing can reveal the same traits, as if the patterns made by the broom in the dust are turned into words on the page – with the added advantage that these words leave a permanent record which can be returned to for further analysis. And be sure there is no shortage of dust to work with. Our emotional and intellectual lives are full of places we never venture into or, at least, have not visited for a very long time. The key to these places is the pen in our hand, and it might be easier (and more fun) to turn than you think. Take this first exercise, which simply asks us to remember something we did recently. It is not just about remembering, though. There is also an element of invention, because it is generally through the mixture of the recollected and the imagined that writing starts to become interesting.

Exercise: **Memory and Imagination**

Describe a recent journey: all the sights, sounds, and smells you experienced – even your thoughts and feelings if you can remember them. But invent one small detail which, although it did not happen, could easily have done so. Then tell the story of your journey to someone else, and see if they can spot what is untrue.

Something this exercise soon reveals is that even people who travel together will notice different things – try it yourself when you are out with a friend – alerting us to the fact that there is never just one way of seeing. These distinctions are compounded by the element of fiction that by its nature will be more personal. One consequence of this is that, as either storytellers or listeners, we must learn not to rule anything out, which is an important lesson both for writing and for life generally. I recall a workshop on the west coast of the USA where one of the participants told us she had just seen a bear riding in the back of a white pick-up truck on Highway 90 a few hours east of Seattle. The rest of us laughed, confident that we had spotted the deception. In fact, the bear was genuine; it was the colour of the pickup that had been invented, which had actually been red rather than white.

This of course raises an obvious question: what is a bear doing sitting in the back of a pick-up truck? Though we may never know the answer, this shows us that the world is a far more extraordinary place than we normally allow ourselves to consider. Indeed, it would be worth asking how many other 'bears' have passed us without our noticing? Paradoxically, it is the element of invention that helps draw attention to these mysteries, for to change a detail without it seeming too obvious requires an accurate recollection of what actually happened. In effect we are being asked to scrutinize the world and our responses to it much more carefully.

This reminds us that it is the power of observation, not glamorous locations, that ultimately makes a great writer. Raymond Carver begins a short story called 'The Hair' like this:

> He worked at it with his tongue for a while then sat up in bed and
> began picking at it with his fingers. Outside it was going to be a nice

day and some birds were singing. He tore off a corner of the matchbook
and scraped it between his teeth.[1]

What could be more trivial than having a hair caught between your
teeth? But over the next four pages Carver brilliantly explores how a
small irritant gradually becomes a metaphor for larger – even existential – dissatisfactions, suggesting that the same fine-tuned sensibility
which Carver used to write his stories also takes us to the heart of spiritual questioning.

In reality there has never been a day in our lives (and maybe not one
hour or even one minute) when something happened that did not
eventually lead to significant results. However, in the onward rush of
events it is usually hard to see these patterns. This is why we need literature – stories, plays, and poems that we can read and re-read: in
order to present things in a more graspable way. (This is also the value
of meditation: in the simple act of sitting quietly we learn how to slow
and still the mind so that we become more aware in our daily activities.)
Although we may never become a highly acclaimed author like
Raymond Carver, it is still true that in developing a writing practice –
the gaze of our awareness focused through the exercises we set ourselves – we have a better chance to find order in the apparent chaos
that surrounds us. Moreover, the decisions we make during this process
– for example the things we choose to omit or include when describing
a journey – tell us a great deal about ourselves. In an important sense
they are what turns a series of events into a story and, eventually, detail
by detail, not just a story but our own life story.

The more we look at these narratives, the more we will understand that
our world – our work, our relationships, the way we live, the way we
sweep a room – is always the result of causes and effects, whether they
are known or unknown. This is no less true of writing than of anything

else we do. Whenever we put pen to paper, each idea will have its subsequent effect – upon us, certainly, as we learn who we are by noting our response to what we have written, but also upon the people and things around us, inasmuch as it shifts to some degree the way in which we respond to them. In this sense, a piece of writing is always the beginning of a new journey: one that not only maps our current experience but also helps us determine the state of mind we are about to move into.

2

The Things We Do Not Bring

Consider for a moment your experience of reading this book. Can you honestly claim that your whole mind is focused on what I am saying? It would be nice to think so, but somehow I doubt it. The truth is that we are like a company of actors inside the one skin. If part of you is excited by what you read, it is likely that another part remains sceptical, and at any sign of discomfort or difficulty this more resistant self will quickly claim centre stage and list all the reasons why starting to write was always going to be a bad idea.

You should not berate yourself for this, however. As anyone who has meditated – tried to keep their mind focused on their breath, for example – soon discovers, this divided and distracted state is the norm. Throughout the day we are being pulled in a number of different or even contradictory directions, but usually we do not allow ourselves the time and space to notice it. And – thinking more positively – to recognize our lack of focus is already an important step in overcoming it. Although it might seem admirable to ignore those dissenting voices and push on regardless, this is to make a premature bid for unanimity as self-doubt still lurks behind us. It is much better to turn round and face the parts of us that we would prefer not to be there; much better to make friends with the wolves that wait at our door.

After all, acknowledging our divisions is not necessarily a capitulation to weakness, nor need it be a negative strategy. I am reminded of the story of how John Cage – who was not only a composer but a lifelong student of Zen Buddhism – finally quit smoking. He began by admitting there were really two John Cages: one that still wanted to smoke and another that didn't. Every time the first lit up a cigarette, the second burst out laughing. It is hard to smoke and laugh at the same time, so within a few days there was only the John Cage who no longer smoked. He realized that to try to break his habit through will-power alone would be to ignore his actual experience. Though this may have worked in the short term it was bound to be unsustainable in the long run. Because freedom is a primary human condition, we will generally only say no to something if we are also free to say yes to it. We need a broader, more inclusive awareness of ourselves, ideally enlivened with humour and a little cunning. 'Tell all the truth, but tell it slant,' was how Emily Dickinson put it.

We should see the next exercise in this light. It addresses the part of us that wants to do something, but it comes at it by first acknowledging the part of us that does not.

Exercise: *Distractions*

Make a list of things you have not brought with you to this writing exercise. (And not just writing, try it whenever you enter any new or difficult situation.)

Just as, in the previous exercise, an invented detail within a journey helped highlight what actually happened, asking what we do not bring to an activity inevitably asks us to reflect on the things we also hope to find there. Here one of our students, Sophia, responds to this question at the start of a week-long writing workshop:

The Things I Didn't Bring

My son
My distraction
Cafetière coffee
Chocolate
My distractions
All my excuses
Everything that holds me back
No videos
No television
Nothing to help me get away from myself
Nothing to buy
No bills to pay
Just me, my book, my pen.[2]

Sophia's list is a good example: no videos, no television, no chocolate: symbols for 'my distractions', whatever it is that usually holds her back.

We sense that Sophia really enjoys writing once she has started, but she rarely gets round to it. Maybe this is partly because we live in a culture of distraction, which makes it hard to prioritize what we should do. All too often we are like someone standing between two gourmet feasts, but starving because of our inabilty to decide which to eat first. There is also the question of personal conditioning. Perhaps we come from a family that did not value the arts, or whose main priority was to have a safe job and a comfortable life. The common view of the writer rarely fits these descriptions.

Yet there are still unexpressed thoughts and feelings under the surface struggling to get out – you need only to consider the play of our dreams to see the abundance of our inner life. And how often do we hear people say – you may be one of them – that they feel sure there is a novel in them if they could just find the time to write. But there always seems to be something more urgent or engaging to snag our attention: bills to pay, the demands of work and family, emails, television – the list is endless.

This is the value of writing exercises. For a time they offer us a bare space – 'just me, my book, my pen,' as Sophia tells us – free from the usual distractions. It is a space where what in everyday life might be dismissed as fantasy or daydream can be seen as experimentation. It is a chance to embrace the wilder parts of us that do not fit our usual persona, and to entice those more wary parts that do not usually come into play. This is not to say it will be comfortable or easy, indeed it may sometimes seem like hard work, but if we just stick with it, without too fixed an idea of what the results should be, the practice of writing takes us to the heart of ourselves and makes it palpable how alive with possibilities we really are.

3

A Wolf at the Door

Exercise: **A Title for Your Autobiography**

Imagine you are about to write your autobiography. Think of a title which, like the title of this chapter, is an image. Be patient: images often take time to surface from the unconscious, so you might need to repeat this exercise several times over the next few days. Keep reflecting on the key events of your life – you could make a list of chapter headings – and trust that something will eventually emerge.

A newcomer to writing recently described her experience of putting pen to paper like discovering a room in your house that you had never been into, maybe a room you did not even know existed, certainly one to which you did not have a key. On the face of it this seemed surprising. Here was a mature self-aware person – a diligent student of Buddhism who had been meditating for a number of years – why should writing apparently be able to achieve something that more conventional spiritual practices could not?

I think the problem lies in the fact that we tend to separate the 'seeker of the truth' (in this case the Buddhist) from the 'dreamer', by which I mean that we tend to discount the part of us that relates to the world through more imaginative and symbolic ways of thinking, relying instead on rational and conceptual formulations of truth or dogma. This is a great loss, for symbols and images offer an opening into intuitions and associations of which our more rational side is barely conscious. As a result they deliver us to knowledge in a directly experiential way. Take the idea of a room in our house we have never been into. We can immediately *see* this because we all have experience of rooms and houses. Because we can see it, we also begin to know what it *feels* like: how frustrating and suddenly strange it is to be locked outside. We are being presented – as Ezra Pound said of the poetic image – with an intellectual and emotional complex in an instant of time.

This power of the image explains why I wanted you to avoid a purely conceptual title for your autobiography. Although the first instinct of the mind is to try to order, in reality our lives are more likely to be a chaos of opposites and contradictions. By being symbolic of the underlying themes, a title built round an image rather than an idea might well present a more honest picture. It is for the same reasons that the writing workshops I co-lead are called 'Wolf at the Door', rather than something prosaic such as 'Writing Workshops Based on Buddhist Practice'. A name like 'Wolf at the Door' invites an imaginative response, the same imaginative response we are encouraging participants to take throughout their life.

What would your reaction be if a wolf came to your door? Except when we visit a zoo, we do not expect to see such untamed creatures any more, certainly not this close to home. They remain in our folk-memory, though, and conjure up thoughts of wildness and the wilderness, a sense of danger yet perhaps freedom as well. Opening the door and finding a wolf outside it would be hard not to feel that something dramatic was about to happen, a sense of anticipation heightened by the wolf being not *by* the door, or *from* the door, but – directly before us – *at* the door. What does the wolf want? Why is it waiting there?

I can tell you my version of this story. For several years pinned to the wall beside my desk was a small piece of paper on which I had written the words 'wolf at the door'. They occurred in the lyrics of a song I was listening to one evening, but I no longer remember why I put them there. Perhaps I thought they would make a title for something, for like most writers I tend to collect good titles. Then, in 1997, after Stephen Parr (or Ananda, to give him his Buddhist name) and I had started to teach workshops together, we decided to give them a name – something that was both eye-catching and intriguing. At the time we were planning our first long and (we feared) arduous teaching tour of North America. To keep our spirits up I said, 'Well at least it will keep the wolf from the door,' meaning, of course, that our trip would bring some welcome income. Without a moment's hesitation Ananda replied, 'But surely we want to keep the wolf at the door?'

We immediately knew we were on to something. That small preposition 'at' perfectly choreographs what we hope to achieve in our workshops: a meeting of worlds, a balancing of opposites – the unmapped wilderness of wolves being brought into relationship with our human domesticity. Symbolically, then, the image of a wolf suddenly appearing at our door presents us with a crucial idea: that for real progress the new and experimental have to be in a fruitful dialogue with the trusted and the familiar. Beyond that, how the 'wolf' and the 'door' are understood will depend upon your disposition. For some it will be a dark sinister wolf approaching a room filled with light – the wolf now being a symbol for what Jung called the 'shadow' or undisclosed side. But for others who tend to be rather gloomy, the shadow might, paradoxically, contain all their banished lightness. Now the wolf becomes a bright radiant snow wolf approaching the dark isolated cabin we have come to call home.

This reversal reveals the value of images: that because they 'show' rather than 'tell' they are open to personal interpretation. Which means that through images we have a very potent mechanism for helping us better to know and trust our inner world. This can be immensely liberating to someone trying to put spiritual teachings into practice, especially if they have a rather narrow and literalistic idea of what the spiritual should be. It is indeed like discovering a room in your home that until now you have never entered.

The symbols and images that emerge through writing are particularly good at healing this sense of the divided self, since they place directly before us aspects of ourselves that we are unable to experience in other contexts. Now we have the means to assimilate the apparently less acceptable emotions and thoughts that, in our eagerness to make progress, we have left by the wayside. As William Blake pointed out, our demons may really be repressed gods, particularly since it is often here that our real (in the sense of authentic) energy is being held. These may be the repressed gods of play, lost in a life too bounded by order and constraint, or they could be the gods of experience – what the Tibetan teacher Chogyam Trungpa called 'the manure of experience' – at the door of any ivory tower in which we try to hide. Or are they the 'gods' of the imagination at the threshold of a life that sought to banish imagination as fantasy and distraction? Only you can say. And your writing may be the first place to say it.

4

Change is Possible

I recently watched a play on television about a young boy coming of age in a London Jewish family. In an early scene we watch him gather up his model planes and banish them to a waste paper basket. But a little later we see him retrieve them and put them back on the window ledge beside his bed. On each occasion nothing is said, yet we have been told a great deal. Suddenly we understand that the boy's know-it-all comments to his parents and older sister are really a front. Behind them lies a lot of unease about his upcoming bar mitzvah, for part of him would prefer to remain with the security of childhood, a security represented by his toys.

I was astounded by the powers of observation these two scenes demonstrated: so much of the boy's internal life revealed in two simple external actions. How had the playwright thought to do this? My answer might surprise you, for I think the key is love. It was, I believe, the novelist Arnold Bennett who said that all great writing has compassion in it. If writers are to appeal not just to our intelligence and our curiosity, but to our feelings and imagination, they must invest their characters with the same qualities. In other words they must care about them, even when they do not particularly like them, for to love is not just to get something, but also to give, and in particular it is to give attention.

To feel love towards all kinds of people is a wonderful idea, but is it simply a matter of temperament whether we can do this, or is it something that can actually be taught? The suggestion that we might educate our hearts as well as our minds is probably alien to most of us.

We tend to believe that our fundamental personality is, like the Ten Commandments, written in stone. Of course we all have our mood swings, but the way we deal with these is surely given at birth, or if not at birth then by a very early age. We might learn to adjust our responses, but not to transform them.

It certainly seemed that way to me until I went to the London Buddhist Centre and learned a meditation called the *metta bhavana* – literally 'the development (*bhavana*) of universal loving-kindness (*metta*)'. This presents us with the idea that we can actually change our basic emotional patterns by encouraging a warmer and more generous attitude both to ourselves and to other people. Starting with trying to feel positive about ourselves, we gradually expand our feelings of loving kindness to include a friend, a stranger, someone we feel antagonistic towards, and finally as much of the world as possible. This expansiveness is important since – like the parable of the loaves and fishes – it suggests that there is always enough metta to go round. There is no limit to positive emotions, apart from those we impose on ourselves. And because we define ourselves by the people we love – they are an extension of who we think we are – the more people we can love, the bigger we become.[3]

To give a taste of how this works, try to enact the development of metta through the following exercise:

Exercise: *Developing Loving Kindness*

In Chapter 3 you were asked to think of a title for your auto-biography. Now try to write a blurb for the back cover. Remember that its purpose is to encourage someone to buy the book, so it should be as positive and interesting as possible – so you are not to be self-depreciatory or cynical. The idea is to celebrate your life and who you are. If you find this difficult, imagine what qualities someone who really cares about you would highlight, then write about these in your own words.

Now repeat the exercise for a near and dear friend. Write a piece for the back cover of their autobiography that rejoices in their positive qualities.

Next choose someone you recognize but do not know, maybe someone who serves you in a shop, drives a local bus, or appears on television. Obviously this step will have to contain quite a lot of invention, but consider what they do, and try to find things you can praise. Or reflect on what sort of person they seem to be and invent some noteworthy things that might have happened in their life.

Next, choose someone you do not particularly like. (If you can't think of anyone close at hand, choose someone from public life.) Remember that the idea is to write something celebratory, so you will have to try to see that person in a different light. One way to do this is to imagine what their loved ones would say about them.

In the meditation itself we end by trying to develop metta towards all four people equally, then gradually expand these positive feelings out to embrace as much of the world as possible. In order to give a flavour of this collectivity, finish by writing a short piece of prose celebrating the town or city in which you live, or the good things about where you work, or an institution to which you belong.

Don't worry if you found the first part of this exercise the hardest, for it challenges a fundamental view that to feel good about other people is acceptable but to feel the same about yourself is selfish, even something to feel guilty about. The truth, however, is the complete opposite: what healthier basis could there be for wishing others well than by wanting the *same for yourself? If not, the stakes are too high and, desperate for the love that we are unable to give ourselves, we fear rejection and withdraw into isolation – the 'prison of self' as W.H. Auden chillingly described it.*

Attempting the metta bhavana meditation quickly highlights how entrenched our emotional life can be. We are inclined to think that if we like some people but not others, that is just the way things are. Yet consider how restricting this attitude really is. It is like setting out on a journey, taking one wrong turning, and then driving further and further in the wrong direction. I suppose we would do this if we believed our car was incapable of being turned round, or if we could not find anyone to ask for directions. And perhaps for similar reasons we believe we have become the victim of our moods and prejudices. No one has ever pointed out the dynamic nature of our mind, or given us instruction in replacing habitual ways of thinking with something more creative.

This was the position I found myself in when I walked through the doors of the London Buddhist Centre in the summer of 1981. I was discontented, but I could not see what to do about it. This had reached its nadir a few months previously when I was nearly killed in a car accident just outside San Francisco. Unsurprisingly, being hurled through a car windscreen was a very traumatic experience. In retrospect, it also left in its wake something extremely positive, for we tend to take life for granted when we are alive, but this becomes much more difficult once we have had a rehearsal for death. Accordingly, after I left the hospital everyone and everything around me seemed to be bathed in radiance, as if it had just emerged from a medieval icon painting. Never before had someone's face looked so beautiful, a flower so vivid, birdsong so delightful. It did not last; the dust of habitual views eventually settled again, but for a short while a door had been opened on to another world.

Objectively it was still the same world I had been in a week earlier, before my accident, so what had changed? Clearly it was my attitude, my state of mind. I had been lucky: life had almost been snatched away from me, but not quite. As a consequence, I had gained a greater appreciation for it. If this fundamental change of perspective could happen once, why could it not happen again? This was a question, we might say, that marked the beginning of my spiritual life.

Fortunately I did not have to keep going through car windscreens in order to transform the way I responded to things. Sitting in the shrine-room of the Buddhist Centre a few months later I felt the door to that other world start to reopen. This time, however, it was not owing to accidents of fate, but through the metta bhavana: a key, as it were, that I could hold in my own hand. Not always, but enough times, as I started to practise meditation, I could feel my attitude to myself and others being modified. This was owing largely to seeing that my emotional states – good and bad – had identifiable causes. For example, I realized I was still harbouring a grudge against an old college friend for not repaying some money he had borrowed when we were students. Since I was never likely to see him again, I saw that I could now choose to think of the money not as a loan but as a gift; then I was free of it. In this way the metta bhavana revealed that it *is* within our power to change our mental states, once we know how, and if we make a consistent effort.

There is a striking testimony to this possibility at the close of Samuel Beckett's dramatic monologue *Krapp's Last Tape*. Krapp is sifting through a ghostly archive of himself as a younger man in the form of a recorded diary. Listening to the 'fool' he took himself for thirty years previously, Krapp has every reason to feel disdain, but just before the last tape runs into silence, he notes,

Perhaps my best years are gone. When there was a chance of happi-
ness. But I wouldn't want them back. Not with the fire in me now.[4]

Like most of Beckett's writing, this is deliberately ambiguous. But one
plausible reading is that Krapp finally grasps the potential – 'the fire in
me now' – of the present moment. It is never too late. It *is* possible to
break free of the endless recycling of tapes – including the tapes playing
inside our heads – by no longer letting those old predictable voices have
their say.

What is true for Krapp is also true for us. We have only to look at old
photographs to see the change that time brings to the physical self. But
the mental self is no less mutable. Just stop reading this book for a
moment, close your eyes, and see how long it is before your mind takes
you somewhere else – it might be the future, or it might be the past.
And how long do these thoughts last? Ideas and feelings come and go,
no more secure than a leaf in an autumn wind.

Although this instability – usually manifesting as a lack of concentration – can be dispiriting, it has a more positive aspect. It shows that
nothing is so fixed about our mental life that it cannot undergo trans-
formation, particularly through the care and attention of the metta
bhavana practice. This means that we don't have to keep embroiling
ourselves in a lifetime's negative conditioning. We can let go of our
current ways of responding to ourselves and others and replace them
with something better, entering a stream of ever more positive
emotions and ever greater creative energy. It ought to be obvious that
this has profound implications for the writing life. If we loosen our grip
on who we think we are, and who we think other people are, we are free
to explore who each of us might yet be. With compassion we can
continually rewrite ourselves.

5

Ideas We Live By

Generally, we have a far more complex mind – both more dark and more light – than we realize. Our writing, by presenting this darkness and light in symbolic or even mythical form, allows us a chance to assimilate them. Here I mean mythical not in the sense of fictitious, but in the positive sense of encapsulating meaning in ways that appeal to both the emotions and the imagination: 'little depth charges into the unconscious', as the painter Aloka has termed the artistic image.

This means that through writing we can start to recognize our core beliefs: the stories we tell ourselves when we think no one else is listening, or when we ourselves are not consciously listening. It is very hard to determine these world-views, particularly if they contradict what we feel we should espouse in public. For example, I might say (as Buddhism has taught me) that everything is in a constant state of flux: life and death, growth and decay. Yet on my way to a meditation class my ageing car breaks down and I suddenly feel angry and betrayed. A small thing, no doubt, but it reveals the divide between my apparent values and the ideas I actually live by: the contradiction that arises when my Buddhism becomes more important than the spiritual process it describes. Humbling though it may be, it is important to recognize this contradiction, since it is only from such reality that things can actually change. The name Buddha, after all, indicates one who is 'awake' – awake to how things really are.

A good way to approach this is through the simple device of compiling a list. If this sounds banal, consider that repetition, like a spell, puts the conscious mind into a sort of trance. Freed from the grammatical constraints of language, what we write can now be produced less by our thoughts and more by our feelings, while the momentum to keep adding to the list is often enough to overrule what we consider to be a more acceptable voice. Here is a poem by Ananda, co-founder of the 'Wolf at the Door' writing workshops, that provides a good example:

Onset

I forget what today is.
I forget to pick up my letters.
I forget I'm on the third floor.
I forget to put tea in the pot.
I forget to ring the damp people.
I forget to put blankets over all the mirrors.
I forget there's a door into the basement.
I forget my father is dead.
I dream all the trees in the wood are his thoughts.
I forget all my dreams.
I forget there's a bridge over the gorge.
I forget I can't walk in the sky.
I forget to order some more memory.
I dream there are no floors in the house and I can see right through to
    the ground.
I forget dreams are lessons.
I forget this has all happened many times before.
I forget this body is a dreaming machine.
I forget I can wake up whenever I want.
I forget all these swaying colours are about to explode.
I forget the only way out is to want a way out.
I forget how to want.
I forget what a day is.[5]

We get the sense that, step by step, the poem is proceeding into more shadowy regions of the psyche – those rooms of our house that we never venture into.

Ananda leaps from one line to another without any apparent connections; although when placed side by side these statements carry a deep emotional undertow. So 'I forget there's a door into the basement' may be no more than fact. Notice, however, what happens when this line is succeeded by:

> I forget there's a door into the basement.
> I forget my father is dead.

Now the door into the basement and the death of his father become inextricably linked. Because we make this step through images rather than narrative and exposition, what this actually means is open to personal interpretation. The poem mythologizes rather than moralizes the stories we each bring to its reading, and such bold statements also remind us that we can only process things via concrete situations, not abstractions. Hence the value, the spiritual value, in the indubitable events of our life: birth and death, love affairs and heartbreaks. These are the ground of our being in which the seeds of our spiritual practice must be sown.

It seems that the reverie of writing a list, whatever its alleged subject, invariably brings us home to what is really on our mind:

> I dream there are no floors in the house and I can see right through to
>   the ground.
> I forget dreams are lessons.

Try it yourself, using Ananda's poem as a model.

Exercise: *List Poems*

Make a list that repeats the following statement, or use something of your own devising:

I believe . . . .
I believe . . . .
I believe . . . .

Set a time limit (no more than ten minutes) and try not to think too hard about what you are saying. Allow yourself to leap from one idea to another as they come to mind and see what emerges. You can always rearrange the statements afterwards if this makes them more resonant.

Making sense is not as important in list poems as touching symbols. When our assumptions have hardened into attitudes, this simple exercise helps us to readopt the more supple stance we had when things were still fresh. The juxtapositions created within the list open out new lines of enquiry, and provide enough contradictory experiences, to remind us – as Ananda had to remind himself – that this body of ours really is a dreaming machine.

6

Lower Your Standards

If we are honest, many of us consider ourselves to be rather lazy, still haunted by those school reports that said 'Must try harder!' So it might surprise you if I suggest that much of what we do comes unstuck not because we don't try hard enough, but because we try too hard, or at least try too hard in the wrong sort of way. We aim too high, too quickly, being prematurely concerned with correctness and results at the expense of practice and process. Since in the short term this offers little chance of success – and it is hard to sustain something we do not feel any good at – we soon feel disheartened and give up before we have really started.

In writing we fall into the trap of believing our prime task is to create 'art', rather than simply put words on the paper and see where they lead. We try to produce the perfect poem, or the perfect story, before we know what it is we are trying to say. Is it any wonder there are so many unfinished novels in the world? In contrast, Ezra Pound observed that people's best writing was often to be found in their letters. Here it is easier just to get on and write since, in a very immediate way, publication is assured as soon as the letter is delivered. And not having expectations about having to produce 'literature', Pound's correspondents simply applied themselves to the matter in hand.

Similarly in meditation. We can believe that unless we experience an immediate flow of positive emotion, or maintain total concentration, we must somehow have failed. We do this because we have an assumption about what someone who meditates *should* be like – an example of the discrepancy between the ideal and the actual that so often trips us up in the spiritual life. It would be much better to attempt something less ambitious and more appropriate to our current level of practice: just keeping someone in mind, say, or noticing when we have drifted out of concentration. This gives us a taste of success which we can build on the next time round. Pain does not necessarily equate to gain, especially if it compounds the negative self-view we are trying to leave behind.

Where does this perfectionist task-master come from? I suspect it is the highly toxic combination of a lack of confidence and a subtle sense of unworthiness. Playing inside our heads is a running commentary continually telling us that we cannot think what we think, or do what we do, because it is either wrong or not good enough: a voice amplified by moral teachings that places all the emphasis on guilt and sin. So instead of wholeheartedly embracing things, as is our birthright, we snatch at life in a sort of smash-and-grab raid before those in authority deem us impostors and ask us to leave, preferably by the back door.

Such inhibitions become so habitual, so familiar, that it might seem to be ourselves talking. In fact it could be the voice of a parent or teacher that we have been carrying since childhood, adults who in all likelihood internalized the same critical voice themselves, so that, from generation to generation, there will be transmitted the lingering trace of what Robert Bly calls, in *Iron John*, 'shame blows':

> Blows that lacerate self-esteem, puncture our sense of grandeur,
> pollute enthusiasm, poison and desolate confidence,[6]

This is shame not in the sense of the realization that our actions have been unworthy of us, but when we are somehow made to feel inadequate as human beings.

Contrast this with a radiant story about the American poet William Stafford as a young boy, whilst bird-watching with his father. As they approached a line of cottonwood trees Stafford's father turned to him and said, 'Now Billy, look carefully, in those trees – you may be able to see the hawk better than I can.' As Bly points out, such a blessing is all too rare in a world where, out of their own sense of inadequacy, parents compete with their children rather than complement them. Perhaps this helps to account for the amazing productivity that Stafford realized in his adult life. He wrote literally thousands of poems. Rising early every morning, he playfully tried out various things in his notebooks, trusting whatever came his way, recalling the tone in his father's voice which seemed to say, 'Maybe you can, maybe you can't … give it a try.'

Here is one small gem from Stafford's vast output:

Note

straw, feathers, dust –
little things

but if they all go one way,
that's the way the wind goes.[7]

We can imagine how Stafford began this as a note to himself, cataloguing his immediate observations about the natural world. It's over in a flash, yet within these few words is formed a whole metaphysics: the weaving of the large with the particular, the inextricable connectedness of things, as the wind becomes a metaphor for conditioned existence – whichever way the wind blows they all will go.

However minutely, our view of the world is changed by reading this apparently casual poem, and surely this is all we should ask of any piece of writing. Yet when he sat down to write I doubt if Stafford had any concern to produce 'poetry'; instead he thought in terms of following his thoughts wherever they led, trying things out rather than holding to previous versions, be it of his writing or himself. For every piece of daily writing that crystallized into a finished work there was another that did not.

When asked in an interview what happened if he hit a block and could not write, Stafford calmly answered, 'I just lower my standards.' Mischievous and provocative, this is surely the best response to the wrongly applied inner critic that we can hope to find. Stafford's friend Robert Bly has described it as one of the most helpful statements about writing he heard in forty years, but I would go further and say it is simply one of the most helpful statements about life. I cannot think of any activity that does not benefit from this approach, especially when we are new to it. Lowering your standards opens up the fixed, blocked, sense of self that says, 'I can do this, but I cannot do that,' and makes us more provisional, more curious, and less afraid.

Writing is a good place to explore the relaxed and open-minded philosophy that Stafford is advocating. Unlike other things we do, such as cooking or driving, nothing very much is at stake. It is just a few ideas on a piece of paper which can be torn up and thrown in the bin if they are not useful. Ideas come and go – like the wind carries straw or feathers or dust – so the next time you sense the inner critic is about to hector you, pick up your pen and begin writing your way across the page. What have you got to lose? Lower your standards and give it a try.

Exercise: *Dialogue with the Inner Critic*

This is an exercise to bring us into dialogue with the inner critic or censor.

Sit quietly and see if you can hear how your critic speaks to you. Does it have a recognizable voice? If so, whose? Are there certain words or phrases that keep repeating themselves? Make a list. Is the voice more strident in some situations than in others?

Do the above exercise several times if you need to. Then using the information you have gathered write a letter from the critic to yourself, listing all the reasons why you cannot do something that is important to you. This will bring the grey and grudging part of yourself into focus, so it might make you squirm.

But having given the critic a voice, write a response listing all your reasons for disagreeing with it.

7

Speaking Better Than We Know

Those who meditate know that the real meditation often begins only when the bell has been rung to signal the end of the formal practice. Suddenly, with nothing to do, we can just let go and be, without judgement or sense of purpose to haunt us. We can have a similar experience during writing exercises: staring at a blank sheet of paper, wanting to write about anything but the given topic. This is why I suggest you set yourself a time limit of ten minutes for most of the exercises in this book. It is long enough to be engaging but not so long that you have a chance to aim for perfection. You will have no choice but to write and see what comes of it. Follow the golden thread, as William Blake urged us to do:

> I give you the end of a golden string;
> Only wind it into a ball,
> It will lead you in at Heaven's gate,
> Built in Jerusalem's wall....

Blake seems to be suggesting that it does not matter which thread you choose; they all lead us eventually to Heaven's gate. It is a path, then, not only of self-knowledge, but also of self-acceptance.

One of the best ways to find the end of a golden string is through 'Ten-Minute Timed Writing', which helps us to write nakedly, even recklessly, with as few constraints as possible. That the purpose is self-expression rather than eloquence or artistry will become obvious as soon as it is described. Something more refined can develop out of timed writing – a number of writers use it as a way of generating new material – but this is not the principal aim, which is simply to put something, anything, on the page, and only then to worry about what it might add up to.

Exercise: *Timed Writing*

Give yourself a subject – it could be something that has been on your mind, a detail from a dream, or a few words taken at random from a book. Write this down and continue writing for ten minutes. It is not a race, so write at your natural speed, but be sure that the pen is moving all the time. This prevents the more censoring mind from overruling whatever it is you happen to say. For the same reason, do not cross anything out. It doesn't matter what you write, or whether you stay on topic, just trust where the thread of your thoughts and feelings takes you. If you get stuck and dry up, write about how this feels, or even keep repeating the same word over and over. Something else is sure to appear eventually.

To give you some idea how this looks on the page, here is an example from a writing workshop held in New Zealand. The subject was 'Doing What I Want'.

Doing what I want means doing the things that are good for me or maybe it's doing the things I think are good for me but then again what I want isn't what's always best for me so I don't know what to do really. Where do I go now this is a strange place to be. I still don't know where I'm going with this and feel I'm running in a bit of a rut but then I suppose life is like that anyway and if I was to do what I want I would be running in a rut anyway so what do I want? I want to not be running in a rut so I must have wants that prevent my running in a rut god the mind can ramble on indefinitely phew! I want to stop. I have stopped, why do I want to stop? Because I don't like the way this is rambling on and not really going anywhere, there's no purpose or direction to it, there's no reality about it and who cares anyway, let's hope I don't keep doing this at other times because that would be incredibly boring and stupid not to say nonsensical. Have I spelt that right and does it matter anyway, who cares! A pause, a pause to think more slowly to let things happen but not to encourage them to go over the top, it's interesting that going slower I'm having a choice of words coming up and I can pick which one I like or want but then that's probably not what the exercise is about and may be defeating the object of the piece, but I also am not sure if there has to be an object to the piece.[8]

This captures the spirit of timed writing very well. The writer stayed with the exercise even when it seemed to be leading him up a blind alley. He was not afraid to repeat himself or resort to clichés. Instead he treated the exercise like a concrete form of meditation – following the mind's interior dialogue as it invents each moment anew. After he read it out it made me realize how much of our inner life is simply a struggle to be authentic.

How would you respond if this was your own timed writing? I would recommend underlining anything that catches your eye: phrases that are particularly mysterious or elegant, or which express something you would not normally allow yourself to say. This may be useful when you come back to the results later, since they can be a fruitful starting point for further writing. Another approach – recommended by the English poet Peter Redgrove – is to not look at the timed writing at all, but put it away and only read it in a week, a month, or even a year's time. When you return to it, you will see it completely afresh. You may even find yourself asking, 'Did I write this?' Such is the way time rewrites us, day after day, year after year.

Lost in concentration we are lost to ourselves, so timed writing becomes a place where the usual restraints do not apply. This often means that – as Peter Redgrove notes – something in us can speak better than we know, what Natalie Goldberg calls, in *Writing Down the Bones*, burning through to first thoughts, 'to the place where you are writing what your mind actually sees and feels, not what it *thinks* it should see or feel'. First thoughts will often have tremendous energy, but they are usually blocked by learned responses and replaced by layers of tamer and more acceptable things: ideas and feelings two or three times removed from the original spark of imagination or insight.

In timed writing nothing is so trivial that it can't be written about. Light is thrown on everything in equal measure. Consequently, an ill-formed piece of timed writing might be much more valuable than any number of 'perfect poems' or 'perfect stories' that we attempt. It can act as a bridge between the ideal and our own experience, the mistakes now becoming part of the path.

It is the sheer physicality of this exercise that keeps us in the realm of spontaneity and freshness. Like an artist making quick sketches, the steady, continuous movement of the pen across the page helps us slip into a reverie of composition. The dance and swirl of each letter as it is formed may even take us back to written language's earliest pictogram origins in the actual world – the capital A, for example, being an (inverted) vestige of the head of an ox. Writing on a computer is less corporeal and probably connects more with the mind than the heart. Computer screens also flatter us to deceive since what we write immediately looks like publishable copy. This may entice us to begin the editorial process far too quickly.

Whenever I got stuck while writing this book I did some timed writing, using as a starting point the subject I was currently working on. As the hand begins to overtake the brain it is amazing how often there emerges a coherent statement of what I had previously been struggling to say. People frequently have dreams that relate back to their timed writings. Both incidents remind us of something that Natalie Goldberg stresses: how the pen – through the hand, arm, and torso – is directly connected to the heart and provides a marvellous link to the riches of the unconscious.

8

Reading Aloud

The Buddha's teachings are only available to us today because for hundreds of years his disciples regularly gathered together to recite them. Several thousand years ago only merchants would have learned to read and write. In India you can still see evidence of the power of the spoken word. Whenever I have visited I have been amazed how a small child in the slums will remember my name. Of course, any European in the middle of a city slum is bound to stand out, but Indians do seem better at committing things to memory than most westerners.

Not so long ago it would have been the same in England. There is a charming story of how, when each new instalment of a Dickens novel was published, it would be displayed in London bookshop windows where rapturous crowds would gather, not to read it – because most of them were illiterate – but to hear it read out by someone who could. The appearance of a crowd of listeners was a sure way for Dickens to know his words had reached their audience.

Today it is less common for writers to read their work aloud. For most of us it is a habit we left behind with childhood. This is a pity because it can be a very effective way to determine whether a piece of writing works. It is hard to hear if the syntax of a story is garbled, or the rhymes of a poem are too laboured, until – like a ship on its maiden voyage – you launch them away from you by reading them aloud. This literally breathes life into our writing and, rather like a painter stepping back from the canvas, also allows us to get a better measure of our progress. It is, in other words, a good way of taking stock.

When I finish a poem I usually go for a walk in some nearby woods. As I wander alone along the pathways, I recite the poem aloud to myself, over and over. This is for me the final part of the writing process, like the fixing after the development of a photograph. I always carry a notebook with me and, after walking for an hour or so, I write down the recited version I seem to have settled on. I do this because I often find the poem I tell myself is not quite the same as the one I wrote back at my desk. This not so much a case of misremembering as actually remembering it better. Reciting the poem out loud allows me to experience it in a new way, noticing any snags in the rhythm, or words that don't quite say – sing would be more accurate – what they mean. As I walk, I am writing with my ears rather than my eyes.

It is better still if someone is listening to you as you recite. Now, like Dickens, you will learn whether your private thoughts match their public response. Even if no one comments it will still have an effect, and start to release you from whatever you have just written. But, you might be thinking, what if the inner critic is inhibiting us from sharing our work with other people – the mere thought of reading aloud already sending shivers along your skin. Well, we can always try lowering our standards, remembering that at the beginning of a writing practice a 'good' piece of writing is simply one that takes us into a more honest and creative relationship with ourselves. To compare is already to fix ourselves and take ourselves too seriously, whereas reading aloud helps to remind us that we are bigger than any one piece of writing, just as we are bigger than anything we do. And as we begin to trust our external voice, maybe we will not fear the critical voice lurking inside quite as much. For this reason I would encourage you to experience a writing workshop or writing group as soon as you can. Through the generous example of others who share their work, it gradually becomes easier for you to do the same.

This decision to share our writing – after perhaps years of inhibition – is one of the most powerful and moving experiences of the writing life. Regardless of the quality of what is read, to take such a step is already an enormous achievement. It confronts head-on the idea that we should not disclose ourselves, or that whatever we say will never be good enough. What better way to overrule this miserable commentary than by reading something out loud? Fortunately, other people rarely give us as hard a time as we give ourselves, so they will be urging us on, even as our own inner critic is urging us to fail.

Students certainly remark that it is the careful listening between participants that is one of the most notable characteristics of Wolf at the Door workshops, though I should make it clear that there is never any pressure on anyone to read out loud, and I suggest this freedom of choice be a touchstone for any workshop you consider joining. Yet although we can see when someone is looking at us, how can we be sure they are listening? For one thing, everyone in our workshops sits in a circle so that we are all facing each other. And anyone who wants to read steps forward and sits in an empty chair – the 'listening chair', as we have come to think of it. It is literally a listening chair for me because, being hard of hearing, I find it useful to position myself next to it. It is also a listening chair for the readers, because as soon as they occupy it they know they will get the people's attention without fear of interruption. Although, to begin with, walking up to the listening chair can seem somewhat daunting, it has the advantage of making the decision to read more conscious. It also focuses us on one person's writing at a time, creating an intimacy so often missing in our daily life.

As we see people in their own right – alone and uncertain just like us – we can become part of a community that abides by different rules. Now our aim is not to dismiss or compete, but to encourage and bring out the best in each other. To help facilitate this we can use the Buddhist model of 'perfect speech', and indeed perfect listening: truthful speech, kindly speech, meaningful speech, and helpful and harmonious speech. As these precepts (though they are better thought of as training principles) make clear, each is balanced by the others. So although it is right to give people an honest assessment of their writing, this should be done appropriately and with awareness. If a comment is to be of value, it must not only be true but also helpful and said with kindness. This is a high ideal and, to the degree it happens, the circle of the writing group becomes a crucible for the trust that is essential for the development of all meaningful relationships.

Moreover, to give voice is not only important for writing but crucial for our well-being. A friend told me recently how, when she first saw her father after he had been diagnosed with cancer, she literally swallowed the grief that welled up inside her. During the ensuing months, as she watched her father decline, she developed a debilitating cough and was frequently lost for words. It was as though she became marooned in sorrow without the healing power of language to rescue her – for the limits of what we can say to others goes a long way to defining our existential solitude. In this case, fortunately, her voice came back, but imagine the consequences of a lifetime spent in mute silence?

Exercise: *Reading Out Loud*

Take a piece of your own writing and read it silently to yourself a few times. Pay particular attention to the vocabulary and syntax: are there certain words or phrases that catch your eye?

Now, to see if the same things also catch your ear, read the piece out loud. Do some things now seem better than before? Or worse? What lessons does this offer for your future writing?

9

Memory Maps

One of the shops in Clifton village, where I live, is an old-fashioned shoe-repairer. In the window is a model of a cobbler. About two feet tall, glasses perched on the end of his nose, he wears a cloth cap and an apron. It is an animated model, and all day long this cobbler knocks a nail into the sole of a shoe. But yesterday he was not moving, his hammer poised in mid-air. As I walked past a small child was staring at the window in some distress. I heard her mother say, 'He's not working today.' It occurred to me that she meant 'working' in both senses – as an electric model and as a cobbler, but I suspect that for the child it could only have had the second meaning. As far as she was concerned the little figure was a *real* cobbler, hitting a *real* nail into a *real* shoe. That was his job. That was what he did when he was working.

The little girl's distress, so palpable as I walked past, reminded me how vivid and immediate a child's world can be, and how it is orientated by such markers as the tiny cobbler in his shop window. He was always there, always working, in the same way that the characters were always there in her favourite books, reassuringly encountered each evening at bedtime. Children love repetition because, in a big strange world, there is so much comfort in predictability. It is also how they learn. (When you think about it, much of what we know is learned through repetition.) This learning is charmed into being because the child takes everything at face value, which means that if a little man swings a hammer he must be alive. And because he is doing this whenever you see him, his reliability makes him a friend.

3

That open-hearted and curious child exists within all of us, even if long put to bed and mostly forgotten. A good way to reawaken him or her is through an exercise that asks us to access childhood memories concretely: by drawing a map of the neighbourhood in which we grew up or somewhere else that was important to us as a child. I got this idea from a high-school teacher friend in America called Vincent Wixon, and he got it from a book by Stephen Dunning and William Stafford called *Getting the Knack*.[9] In this book the exercise is developed through a number of stages, but I will describe a condensed version built around the main element: the drawing of the map.

Exercise: *Mapping Your Childhood*

Draw a map of the place where you grew up as a child. Make the map as large and as detailed as you can, with colours to differentiate things. Put in streets and their names, houses and the people who lived in them, shops, factories, schools, and other buildings; and note important natural elements such as trees and rivers. You could also mark where the sun rose and set, your favourite places, magical locations, areas where you played or escaped to, and those haunted spots where you never dared to venture. Try to reach beyond the visual. Make a note of sounds, smells, tastes and textures: all the things that gave the place its particular atmosphere.

If you find the memories of childhood painful then choose a later time in your life. You can always work back to earlier experiences gradually.

Then use the map as the basis for a piece of writing. Keep this actual and concrete by using as many names and physical details as possible.

It has been said that the mind of a child is like a pond into which each and every experience is dropped. The pond eventually becomes so full that things start breaking through to the surface. But, since one experience is built on another, nothing is lost, we just have to dive down into the pond to find it again. One means of doing this is via the senses. For example, I am sure we have all had the experience of suddenly being transported back somewhere by a smell such as baking bread or burning wood. Smells are all pervasive and would have certainly created a strong atmosphere during our childhood, yet they are now largely unconscious, which means they can by-pass the adult and conceptual mind and plug us directly into the past.

This exercise works in a similar fashion. If we go into enough detail, drawing the memory map can be an almost visceral experience, as much akin to dreaming as it is to thinking. Certain things will immediately stand out from the map because of the sensual and imaginative connection we made with them all those years ago. Doing the exercise myself, I recalled how, when I was five years old, we moved house and my parents told me our new neighbour was a widow. I did not know what a widow was; it sounded like 'window' but I felt sure it must be connected with darkness and witches. But Mrs Hill turned out to be a kind and welcoming neighbour and her three children soon became good friends. I thought I had forgotten this, but then I drew the memory map and it all came flooding back.

Like some half-remembered fairytale, that fearful association with 'widow' was still lurking deep in my memory. In one way or another it was continuing to colour my life. It is largely the past that makes us what we are today, and I am convinced it is only by intentional recall that we are finally released from that past. We can only really let go of something once we have brought it back to consciousness as vividly as possible. This is the value of an exercise like the memory map, which allows us to set up a creative dialogue between different phases of our experience. But because the framework is the 'actual objects in your life' (as Stephen Dunning and William Stafford put it) we can do it without fear of becoming too self-indulgent. It is an imaginative leap from 'here and now' to 'once upon a time', that magical realm where so much of what we now take for granted originally came into being.

10

The Curse of Originality

Sunday Morning

Impending doom in the shape of Mrs Nicholl - Sunday school teacher. Waking up dreading the morning ahead. Fuelled with all the indignation a five-year-old can muster.

'But you don't go to church, so why should I?'

'So you don't end up like me,' says my father, still relishing his freedom after a childhood of enforced choir practice and services at the local Welsh chapel three times on the Sabbath.

It's not so much the tedium, as the wait afterwards. He's always late, Dad. He gets distracted car washing or, worse still, car mechanics, so when I finally did get back home there'd be splashes of oil and bits of car engine discarded on the drive.

So I'm stood waiting outside the gate, the last child, knowing if I start to walk I'll get to the dual-carriageway, and that way terror lies.

What if he forgets me altogether? What if he can't get the car started?

Then I'll have to cross the thundering road, alone. Again.[10]

This powerful reminiscence was written towards the end of a week's writing workshop held at Rivendell, a Buddhist retreat centre in the south of England. Just a few days earlier Sharon, its author, had been convinced she would never create anything worthwhile, certainly not when compared to all the 'brilliant' work being produced by other participants. This was surprising, because for many years Sharon had been a journalist. She had made her living from writing, something most of us at Rivendell could only dream about.

So where did 'Sunday Morning' come from? Clearly it is a highly engaging evocation of the world of a five-year-old, but it is also – though this is not so apparent – a direct response to another piece of writing: a sonnet by Louis MacNeice also called 'Sunday Morning'. Knowing this, other parallels become clear. MacNeice's abstract Man 'tinker[ing] with his car' becomes Sharon's father washing his car or being distracted by car mechanics. And MacNeice's

> But listen, up the road, something gulps, the church spire
> Opens its eight bells out,[11]

perhaps reminded Sharon both of the impending doom of Sunday school, and her father's enforced choir practice at the local Welsh chapel.

But despite these borrowings this is no mere replication. A sonnet has been transformed into a piece of prose, and, moreover, prose that is deeply personal. Although MacNeice's poem provided the impetus, the result is charged with the originality of actual experience. We also sense a reconciliation taking place between adulthood and childhood, between the now of Sharon's perception, and the then of her recollection. And within this reconciliation might be glimpsed – hence the writing's moral and spiritual value – the way things could be different in the future.

How, then, did Sharon get to such artistry from the impasse of believing she had nothing worthwhile to say? It happened because she was willing to draw from her own experience – 'going home' as Natalie Goldberg calls it. Earlier in the week Sharon had not given herself the chance to do this. Instead she had been comparing her writing with other people's, convinced that she could never measure up to it. This is something we all do: rather than accept the experience we are having, we want something else, something better or more interesting. So someone tells us about what has happened to them and we think, 'Oh yes, that's what I want. I want an experience like theirs.' In doing this, of course, we reject ourselves.

Paradoxically, Sharon finally overcame this by allowing herself to use someone else's writing as a starting point – the nature of the exercise being to write something that grew out of a study of MacNeice's sonnet. Although this might look like comparison, it is really more akin to appreciation – both of MacNeice and of herself. Sharon met something in MacNeice's poem that sparked a connection with her past and allowed her to pattern it in a new way. Writing now became not a question of rejecting her experience but of organizing it.

To someone with a background in journalism this could seem like a betrayal. Surely 'creative' writing is not about recollections, but about being original and inventive? But that raises a question: where do these qualities come from? The seventeenth-century philosopher and historian Giambattista Vico tells us, 'Imagination is memory rearranged.' Several hundred years later, Katherine Mansfield suggested the way to art was through intensification of the memory. Both these statements challenge too narrow an understanding of originality by reminding us that – since existence is always wholly dependent and conditioned – nothing can be created without reference to something else. There *is* nothing new under the sun: every thought and idea, just like everything we do, is the progeny of all that has gone before.

Consider, for example, Louis MacNeice writing 'Sunday Morning'. It is likely that his first impulse as a poet was the inherent music of language – the 'music of what happens' is how Seamus Heaney has described it: the rise and fall in pitch and accent of words which gradually coalesced into the poem's opening lines:

> Down the road someone is practising scales,
> The notes like little fishes vanish with a wink of tails,

But – if Heaney is right – this is not just music but the music of *what happens*. That is, well-sounded experiences that are either a direct report of events – for perhaps someone was actually practising on a musical instrument as MacNeice wrote – or modelled on things that lead back to actual events: actual roads, and actual fishes, that MacNeice has seen or heard about and now recalls in his writing. In the same way, we as readers make sense of the poem's images by forming little pictures in our minds based on our prior knowledge of the world.

Similarly when reading the first sentence of Sharon's piece of writing: 'Impending doom in the shape of Mrs Nicholl – Sunday school teacher.' We will all bring our own particular flavour to 'doom', and construct an image of Mrs Nicholl from figures in our own lives. And remember that when Sharon wrote that line she went through the same process. Mrs Nicholl was not actually present, so she had to be conjured up from memory. It is this conjuring up – an act of the imagination that occurs whenever we recall something not immediately before us – that links the reading and writing of newspapers to memoirs and to poems. The difference is one of degree, not kind.

To consider that originality (the curse of originality is what a theatre director friend of mine calls it) should be the aim of a writing exercise is to be doomed before you start. Indeed, this could even be the impending doom that Sharon intuited as a child, and which all these years later she has finally found a way to write about. All the weight of guilt and sin – and the terrible lack of self-confidence that comes with it – rained down upon us on childhood Sunday mornings because we were led to believe we were not perfect. Sharon had sought to escape from this memory through the fantasy of originality, but was then haunted by the idea of this strategy's failure. How much better to borrow from her own life experiences and imitate and learn from someone else's writing. This was not ceasing to be herself, but ceasing to be limited by it.

Exercise: *Borrowed Writing*

Open a novel or a poetry book at random and write down one or two paragraphs of prose or a short poem, or part of a poem. Underline anything that makes a direct connection with your own experience – it could be a place, a name, a sequence of events, or a mood or atmosphere. Gather all these details together and see if you can turn them into a piece of writing of your own. It doesn't matter if a poem becomes prose, or vice versa. And don't worry if many of the ideas seem borrowed, for even if the things you start with are not your own, your responses to them will be.

11

Less is More

If I tell you that I grew up in a small town called Ware – on the River Lea in Hertfordshire, about twenty miles north of London – what does this reveal about the following poem?

Childhood

When I stepped
across the secret
river
evening was sure to follow.

It is in fact an acrostic, one of the many poetic forms that delight in demonstrating that by restricting our choices we sometimes gain more than we lose.

Because it works within tight parameters, several of the questions we have to ask when we write a poem are already answered if we choose to write an acrostic: where to begin, for a start; where to break the thought patterns for another; and – most fundamentally – how many lines we will end up with. A clue to how this works is given by the echo of 'across' in its name. But if you are still puzzled – and that is another clue – the dictionary definition of acrostic tells us all we need to know in order to write one: 'a poem or puzzle in which the first letters of each line spell a word or sentence'.

Now, if it was not obvious already, you can see that the first letters in my poem form the name 'Ware':

> When I stepped
> Across the secret
> River
> Evening was sure to follow.

Whenever I think back to my childhood, my mind sooner or later turns to the River Lea. ('Ware' comes from the Old English for 'weir'.) It ran through the town park where my father worked as a gardener, it was where my friends and I rode our bikes or tried our hands at fishing, and it was later where we first tried our hands at courting. So, given that Ware was to be the subject, it soon became clear that the penultimate line of my acrostic should make the word 'river', and then, my thinking continued, why not give the word 'river' that line to itself just to bring the point home? After that it was rather like doing a crossword – the puzzle element being there as much for the writer as for the reader – trying to find things that fitted around this now complete third line.

For me, the Lea was a magical, secret place, particularly at twilight – when 'evening was sure to follow' – as I walked alongside it on my way home from school. The river became a divide between two worlds: the bright and boisterous school day filled with my friends, and the more solitary evening when I would sit at home playing the piano and teaching myself to write music. (It was song-writing that first led me to poetry.) Not that I consciously planned the poem to be about this. One of the gifts of poetry is the way its structures – 'blessed structures, plot and rhyme' as the poet Robert Lowell called them – create their own momentum, the consequence of this being that poetry is probably the most intuitive form of writing there is.

Although I did not have an intellectual idea of what the poem was trying to achieve, I did have a strong emotional theme. And because 'Ware' is such a short name, I did not have much room to play with. So I had no choice but to try to capture the essence of my thoughts in one strong magical image which – less being more – all poems should aim for anyway. After that it was largely a matter of trial and error, letting my memories search for the right metaphor, guided by the form itself, i.e. that I happened to live in a town whose name had four letters – not too much trial or error as it happened, for looking back in my notebook I find I arrived at the finished poem in very few drafts.

This ease almost certainly came about because a particular type of relaxation takes place when we know that certain things have to happen at certain times – for instance, a line can only be so long before the next letter of the acrostic starts to assert its claim. To some extent the loss of formal freedom allows for greater freedom in the composition itself, acting as a kind of spur that obliges us to take risks and try things that we may never have thought of in other circumstances. Not just linguistic risks but emotional ones too. I have noticed that because the rational mind is preoccupied with the pattern making, the feelings are able to slip in, as it were, by the back door. So the acrostic can be a surprisingly rich and emotionally satisfying form with which to experiment.

Exercise: *Acrostics*

Write an acrostic about somewhere important to you. Start by writing the place name vertically and build the lines out from it. If the name consists of more than one word, leave a space between each word to indicate a new stanza. For example, Glasgow would give one stanza of seven lines, whereas San Francisco would produce two stanzas, one of three lines followed by another of nine.

Be sure to write about the place you have chosen so that the poem becomes a marriage of the external verbal formula and your inner response to the place name.

The lines can be of any length, some long, some short, even a single word. Avoid making every line just one word, as this diminishes the puzzle element inherent in the form; it also means you lose an opportunity to experiment with where and when to break a line, which is one of the most characteristic devices of poetry. For the same reason try not to choose words arbitrarily just to complete the form. You are ideally seeking words that not only fit successive letters of the name but also develop what you want to say.

People's names also provide a good starting point for acrostics.

It is worth asking about your response to this more formal type of writing exercise. Speaking personally, one of the great delights of writing poetry is the discipline of matching form to content. I love the way it helps me to guide my thinking in more elegant and eloquent directions. I am reminded that when asked where he got his ideas W.B. Yeats replied, 'Looking for the next rhyme.' Although this might seem like intellectual abdication, it is surrender to a deeper unity by letting our more intuitive emotional intelligence – not to mention serendipity – also play a part.

Ideally we should take a form such as the acrostic and reinvent it so that it allows us to articulate what we want to say, and in the process re-invent ourselves – in the sense of being guided away from habitual ways of expression. This means respecting the structure, but not at the expense of our individuality.

There is a parallel here with spiritual teachings. It is all too easy to feel these are imposed from outside: external forms which, disconnected from our needs, do not take us into account. But any view of morality, for example, is not going to be sustainable if we expect it to fit us like an off-the-peg jacket. We need to make the teachings our own, not by de-valuing or ignoring them but by tailoring them to fit the unique shape of our individual circumstances.

Writing can help us in this by showing how to use limitations and restraints more playfully and creatively. It will give us concrete ex-amples of the outer discipline becoming one with our inner responses, such as when the right word suddenly matches the next letter in an acrostic. This reveals how an outcome can be so intrinsic and correct that – regardless of the means that brought it about – we no longer wish it to be any other way.

12

Beginnings, Middles, and Ends

As the acrostic demonstrates, verse thrives on limitations; this is the way it articulates itself. But prose is inherently more discursive; consequently any attempt to limit it tends to feel contrived, but this does not mean it isn't useful to try. Having to weigh the value of each individual word can be a very good exercise, likely to test the worth of many of the things we intended to say. In fact, most of us already have a precedent for this editing process: whenever we tell a joke we instinctively know to trim our language so that the emphasis falls on to the punchline.

The most obvious way to limit a piece of prose is by restricting the page size or the number of words. For example, you could write something that exactly fills a given space: perhaps a page of your notebook or the computer screen, or even a scrap of paper torn at random. When restricting the word count you simply set an arbitrary limit and use only that number of words. In either case – by folding the paper in half or by halving the number of words – it is worth investigating how far you can reduce the writing before it ceases to make sense. This brings home the truth that for the writer the medium *is* the message: it is literally all there is between you and your reader.

A more conceptual approach is to limit the content rather than the form. One way is to try to write a piece of prose without using adjectives or adverbs. Or, pushing this line of thought even further, writing something without using one of the vowels. Although this may feel more like a game of Scrabble than a piece of writing, it is a valuable lesson in how language shapes our thinking and thereby determines our world, reminding us that words think us as much as we think them.

All these exercises become more interesting if you use them to write a narrative rather than a piece of descriptive prose. Now a tension is created between the needs of characterization and plot and the resources available to express them. As choices about your language compete with choices about what you want to say, you are forced to become more inventive – even adopting writing strategies you've never used before – because if you are going to write a narrative there is one element that can never be discarded: something has to happen. For a story to be a story there has to be a beginning, a middle, and an end – which means, as Margaret Atwood has pointed out, there has to be a clock ticking.

Consider a postcard from a far away island. If all it describes is the weather, it is simply a report. But if it adds that there are only a few hours before a hurricane arrives, the recipient will now have a story on, or even *in*, their hands. There is now a race against time, meaning that between the play of language (on the card) and the play of the world (on the island) lies the human dilemma of our impermanence – just as, however well disguised it may be, the shadow of the clock (the shadow of death), hangs above everything we do. That is why there are no new stories, change being the only thing about existence that does not ever change.

I recently saw the truth of this while sitting on a bus in Edinburgh. It was during the evening rush-hour, and the journey from Leith into the city centre was very much a stop-and-start affair. As the bus was about to turn from Dublin Street into Princes Street the traffic lights turned from green to red. To my amazement, the driver got up from his seat and went to a small locker by the door. Having taken out a new ticket-roll he proceeded to walk back towards us in the bus. (On Edinburgh buses you pay the driver but collect your ticket from a machine by the stairs.) Quite nonchalantly he put the new ticket-roll into the machine before walking back to his seat, just in time to pull away with the rest of the traffic.

The amount of tension this generated in me was amazing: it could have been a scene from an Alfred Hitchcock film. It was not that the driver showed any particular concern, since it was probably a manoeuvre he and his colleagues performed regularly. Although the whole incident took only a minute or two, it seemed like an age as I stared through the front window of the bus, wondering when the lights were going to change to green.

Would it have mattered if the lights had changed before the driver got back to his seat? Probably not; after all, the traffic was hardly about to rush off anywhere. Nevertheless the countdown imposed by the traffic lights immediately created a drama. I unexpectedly found myself in a story – a beginning, middle, and as yet unknown ending – played out against the red, amber, and green of the traffic lights, a sequence that put a time-frame around things and, as such, distilled these moments down to something more essential, even existential.

This is the value of limitations. They are a reminder that we cannot live on our terms alone. They are a rehearsal for the final drama that somewhere on the road ahead awaits us all. Once you've got clocks ticking you also have time passing, and time is colour-blind: it never sees red or amber lights, only the green one which is forever beckoning it on.

Exercise: *A Short, Short Story*

Think of a number between 100 and 200. Now write a story that is exactly this number of words long. In this exercise a miss is as bad as a mile, so whether your story is one word too long (or too short) or ten makes no difference; you will have to rework it until you get the exact number. Remember this is a story you are writing, not just descriptive prose, so something has to happen; there has to be a clear beginning, middle, and end.

This exercise is a good example of the use of editing to help us clarify things. Limiting our resources makes us progress much more incrementally, which inevitably leads us deeper into the experience we are trying to describe. With so few words available to us we have no choice but to decide what it is we really want to say.

13

Chance, Magic, Luck

The next exercise is very good if you tend to be cautious. It throws caution to the wind by introducing an element of chance, and maybe a touch of magic and luck too. Chance means surrendering yourself to forces outside your control – to be, we might say, a disciple of the unknown, not just the things we know. You might wonder how you could bring chance into writing and still make sense, but it is quite simple: all you need is pen and paper and a dice or some playing cards. The exercise is called 'making new similes' because it plays with this figure of speech, but it is not so much an English class as a linguistic lucky-dip.

Exercise: **Making New Similes**

Complete the following similes.

As happy as . . . .
As sad as . . . .
As dark as . . . .
As hard as . . . .
As red as . . . .
As confused as . . . .
As soft as . . . .
As blue as . . . .
As small as . . . .
As dead as . . . .
As lonely as . . . .
As high as . . . .

Write them out as a list, and number each one. For example:

1. As happy as a lollipop
2. As sad as a dead bird
3. As dark as the cupboard under the stairs
4. As hard as a disillusioned man
5. As red as the ball flying over the wall
6. As confused as a horse in a one-horse town
7. As soft as a favourite pillow
8. As blue as a saxophone's note
9. As small as a needle in a haystack
10. As dead as neglect
11. As lonely as a lost dog
12. As high as the last apple on the tree

Next, lay five playing cards numbered from 2 to 6 face down before you. (You could also use the roll of a dice, or five pieces of paper with numbers written on the underside.) Turn over one of the cards. The number that appears becomes the organizing principle over your list of similes. For example, if you turned over a 5, then the ending of line 1, 'a lollipop', drops down five places to become the ending of line 6 (1 + 5 = 6) which originally read, 'As confused as a horse in a one-horse town', meaning the new simile will be 'As confused as a lollipop'.

Doing this for each line in turn produces:

Beginning 6 + Ending 1 = As confused as a lollipop
Beginning 7 + Ending 2 = As soft as a dead bird
Beginning 8 + Ending 3 = As blue as the cupboard under
the stairs
Beginning 9 + Ending 4 = As small as a disillusioned man

Beginning 10 + Ending 5 = As dead as the ball flying over the wall
Beginning 11 + Ending 6 = As lonely as a horse in a one-horse town
Beginning 12 + Ending 7 = As high as a favourite pillow
Beginning 1 + Ending 8 = As happy as a saxophone's note
Beginning 2 + Ending 9 = As sad as a needle in a haystack
Beginning 3 + Ending 10 = As dark as neglect
Beginning 4 + Ending 11 = As hard as a lost dog
Beginning 5 + Ending 12 = As red as the last apple on the tree

If one of the results catches your imagination, use it as the basis of a piece of writing. For example, what might be the story of the horse in a one-horse town? How did it come to be there? What did it do all day? Will it ever find a companion?

One of the charms of this exercise is that it doesn't matter how clichéd your original choices are because they will get thrown into confusion as soon as the element of chance is introduced. Some of the results will be strange or absurd; others will be more felicitous. Take 'as small as a needle in a haystack'. Although this is a play on the common expression 'looking for a needle in a haystack' it is not much more than a variant. However, after turning over card number 5 this was transformed into 'as sad as a needle in a haystack': not a particularly dramatic change but what a beautiful difference it makes. We are suddenly asked to look at things from the needle's point of view, and I am not sure I had ever thought to do that before. Think how lonely it must feel to be lost in a haystack with only a million to one chance of being found and re-united with your needle friends.

This exercise is also a brilliant way of lowering your standards. No self-respecting writer would have dared touch the idea of a needle in a haystack with, dare I say it, a barge-pole. But what better place is there to start with such a cliché than in the process of constructing new simi-les, since it gives us the opportunity to reawaken the wisdom that makes a cliché so popular in the first place. We are being helped to ex-perience the familiar in an unfamiliar way, which – if you stop to think about it – is what the Buddhist goal of Enlightenment is said to be.

Whether or not we find it easy to surrender control to the playing cards will reveal something about our fundamental relationship to the world. To the optimists it would have presented little or no problem, their basic attitude being that life is a constant stream of possibilities anyway. For the pessimists, however, this exercise will be more challenging, since the idea of luck will almost certainly mean bad luck. Fortunately our personal disposition has no bearing on the final result. Whatever our stance, fate is taken out of our hands and placed in those of chance. Consequently we are given a taste of how writing can open us up to creative influences bigger and less fathomable than the conscious mind. We can either see these influences as our own latent potential or as something gratuitous in the universe, but this is less important than becoming receptive to them so that they can play their part in every-thing we do. Then we are learning to live within life's mystery and our own complexity.

I suspect these influences are akin to what in the arts we think of as 'inspiration' or, if we wish to personify it, our muse. In truth, I am not sure it is possible to make real progress without having a degree of faith in such a force, even if we do not consciously relate to it in these terms. Think how feeble the pen would seem, and how unending the paper, otherwise. Whether we relate to such positive supra-personal forces abstractly as Beauty, Truth, or Enlightenment, or as archetypal figures who represent qualities we seek to develop, the important thing is that they are bigger than we are. They bring a gift which is dependent not on our volition alone but also on our receptivity to a kind of sympathetic magic across time and space that helps both to console and to inspire.

It seems a long way from such radiant figures to a lonely horse in a lonely town, but the chance riches of the new similes remind us that we cannot proceed from the rational to the intuitive by increments alone, since, being completely different modes of perception, they need to be developed in completely different ways. Sometimes it is wise to surrender to things beyond our control, to become what might be thought of as willingly lost, as we do momentarily in this exercise.

14

Show, Don't Tell

W.B. Yeats notes in his poem 'High Talk' that 'Processions that lack high stilts have nothing that catches the eye.' What catches our eye is the unusual – in this case people high above the ground – and that jolts us from expectations about the world. Presumably most of us waiting for the parade will never have lifted ourselves onto stilts, so, when we catch sight of these elongated people, our heart – which is to say the child's heart still lurking within us – misses a beat because we suddenly imagine what it would be like to have such long legs. That invariably means entering into a different relationship with ourselves. Now all sorts of questions race through our minds. What do we look like down here? What sights can the stilt walkers gaze upon that we cannot? How do they put on their socks? The strange 'Daddy-long-legs upon his timber toes' catches our eye because it captures our imagination. We have entered another realm.

I saw a striking example of this in the National Gallery of Scotland in Edinburgh. I was looking at a painting called 'Francesca da Rimini', by the nineteenth-century Scottish painter William Dyce, which illustrates an episode from Dante's *Divine Comedy*. It is a portrait of the young lovers Francesca and Paolo sitting on a terrace while the Moon and Venus (appropriately enough) rise above them. The rather ardent Paolo is stealing a kiss as Francesca gazes demurely down at the ground – as well she might, since she is married to Paolo's older and much less attractive brother Giancotto. In the original painting Dyce depicted Giancotto to the left of the lovers, creeping up to murder them. However, in a rather bizarre twist, in 1882 (by which time Dyce had been dead for eighteen years) that part of the canvas was damaged and had to be cut away. But not entirely. Careful scrutiny reveals that gripping the parapet of the terrace are three fingers of Giancotto's left hand.

Inadvertently, this wonderfully demonstrates the famous writing adage, 'Show, don't tell.' To see Giancotto about to strike would no doubt have been poignant – his deformed rage contrasting with the sublime young lovers – but to glimpse those fingers is much more disturbing. They are a portent of what is about to happen but one that our imagination must flesh out. To paint the whole of Giancotto would, in writing terms, be simply to state that he is angry. But his disembodied hand becomes a symbol for a drama that we enact in our mind's eye, equivalent not just to telling us that Giancotto is angry but actually involving us in his angry experience.

Experiences and symbols are personal in a way that abstractions such as anger are not. As the painting now stands, each of us must imaginatively create Giancotto and thereby entwine him with our intimate knowledge of similar dramas. As Yeats suggested, it is the surprising – in this case those ghostly fingers – that best captures the imagination. It is also true that the imagination captures the surprising. Why is that hand there? What is about to happen? This has important implications for our spiritual life because, if it is to stay fresh, it will need the imaginative and the unexpected; it is these which carry us from the realm of religious thought into the realm of religious feeling.

To try to develop qualities such as pure awareness or total compassion is clearly a momentous undertaking and one that could easily overwhelm us. This is where the leaps of the imagination that we learn to work with in our writing can be particularly effective. So when we recite devotional verses or perform rituals – practices to help us 'surrender' our control, as I mentioned in Chapter 13 – we can try 'acting as if':

an imaginative response that allows us to state the ideal as if it is the expression of states of mind we have already experienced. Consider that circus stilt walkers 'act as if' they really are ten feet tall, and trapeze artists 'act as if' they really can defy gravity. If they did not have this faith they would soon hit the ground. Similarly we should try to say the words of rituals as though we mean them, as though we already see our-selves acting in the way they suggest. As a preparation for this, when-ever we pick up our pen, or turn on our computer, we could write 'as if' we already have major work behind us. Try this and see whether it makes a difference. Even if nothing changes immediately, it is planting a positive seed.

In one of the Buddhist rituals I regularly perform there is a verse called 'Rejoicing in Merit', which begins:

> I rejoice with delight
> In the good done by all beings,
> Through which they obtain rest
> With the end of suffering.
> May those who have suffered be happy.[12]

However well intentioned we are, each of these statements will remain an abstraction unless brought to life through the engagement of our imagination. Remembering the 'show, don't tell' formula, I find a good way to prompt this is to 'see' the meanings as well as simply say them – 'see it feelingly' as Gloucester says in *King Lear*. I try to see 'rejoice' – its look upon someone's face and then my own; see 'delight' – a crowd of people laughing and applauding; see 'the good done by all beings' – a nurse in a hospital, a teacher in a school, my own acts of kindness. Of course it would be too laborious to do this with everything we say, but at least key images can be brought to life in this way. After a while it becomes an established state of mind, helping us to recite the words as if we mean them.

Whether through writing or through ritual, it is important to create arenas for ourselves where these imaginative practices can flourish. All too often in our daily lives the fantastic and the visionary – the acting 'as if' – is overtaken by the utilitarian. As Yeats notes in his poem, 'some rogue of the world' has stolen the stilts to 'patch up a fence or a fire'. We need to raise our sights and let the imagination take effect, which means putting our scepticism to one side and acting as if we really do rejoice with delight and seek the end of suffering; as if we really can, like the stilt-walker, experience the world from a different perspective, which means showing – not telling – people the results of our aspirations by seeing them for ourselves in our mind's eye.

Exercise: *Building Up Pictures*

Take a picture from a magazine and cut it into strips about an inch wide. (It is best if the picture has a number of elements to it and is not just a close-up of one thing.) Working from left to right add one strip at a time to build up the picture. Each time you reach a stage that creates an interesting image in its own right, write about it. One way to do this is to treat it as a scene in a novel or a film and imagine what happened immediately before, or just after, the image in front of you.

15

On the Other Hand

Exercise: *Opposite Handwriting*

Write your name and address with the hand you don't normally use. (If you are ambidextrous, choose your weaker hand, and try not to look at the paper as you write.) What does this feel like? Does your opposite-hand-writing suggest anything about you that you have not noticed before?

If you want to take this further, write a dialogue between your weaker hand and your usual writing hand:

Usual writing hand asks weak hand what it wants.

Weaker hand answers.

Stronger hand responds.

And so on. You could also keep an opposite-hand journal for a week and see what it reveals.

It has been said that if you could become another person for even a few moments you would probably become Enlightened. So strong is our attachment to the idea of who we are that even the smallest jolt out of it can have a immense effect. This is one of literature's great gifts: poetry, fiction, and drama all allow us to see the world through someone else's eyes. This is an illusion, of course, because ultimately we will always overlay the writer's world with our own, and filter their voice through our own. Nonetheless, it remains one of the best openings we've got.

Take these lines from a poem by Philip Larkin called 'The Building' – a hospital, although it is never identified as such, as if to remind us there is something unspeakable to modern society in its purpose:

> Every few minutes comes a kind of nurse
> To fetch someone away: the rest refit
> Cups back to saucers, cough, or glance below
> Seats for dropped gloves or cards.[13]

Time and again another patient is beckoned, and the rest, still un-called, do everyday – though suddenly futile – things such as refitting cups to saucers. This is a fine example of a writer 'showing, not telling'. The overall mood is one of doom and disconsolation, but it is created purely through activity and gestures – things so ordinary and tangible that we cannot help but identify with them ourselves. As we read, the anxiety of the patients in 'the building' becomes a rehearsal of our own discomfort in the face of sickness and death. Through such acts of the imagination we are brought into sympathy with other people's plight and with our own. It is in effect the same mutual concern that we are aiming for in the metta bhavana (development of loving-kindness) meditation that I described in Chapter 4.

There are also other people waiting within us, inasmuch as we all have aspects of our character that we choose to hide, or simply do not know very much about. A good way to contact these other selves is to do something extremely familiar but in an unfamiliar way. The key to this is, as the exercise suggests, right here in my hand: I am writing this quite naturally with my left hand, but what happens if I join the majority of you and start writing with my right? Well quite a lot actually. When I began to write my name and address a remarkable thing happened, for what tentatively and laboriously scratched its way onto the page was:

David Keefe, 16 Croft Road ...

But wait a minute, I do not live at 16 Croft Road any more, and these days I generally think of myself by my Buddhist name, Manjusvara. Remarkably, and completely unconsciously, as soon as I tried to write with my right hand, I found myself back in my childhood identity and childhood home: the time and place that I first learned to read and write.

Other people who have done this exercise have reported similar awakenings. One man became quite distressed – and remember that all he was doing was writing out his name and address – by the indelible feeling that he was recovering from a stroke and having to relearn all his writing skills again. Another workshop participant, a mother, suddenly felt what it must be like for her nine-year-old son to take so long to write things out and express himself. The exercise builds empathy, making us more aware of our shared vulnerability in the face of what Larkin calls in his poem 'the coming dark'.

So much of what we do is habitual. Through repetition it becomes hard-wired into the very circuitry of our being. Eventually we have already anticipated most aspects of our life and we increasingly stop being surprised by ourselves – hence our discomfort with new and embarrassing situations. (The curious and mischievous wolf no longer comes to our door.) But by picking up a pen in the opposite hand some kind of reformulation takes place. A minor shift of response creates a major change in our perception. Struggling to form each letter of each word we find ourselves once again held in the act of writing itself. Like encountering a creature we long thought banished or even extinct, we have started to meet that mystery which is the other side of ourselves.

16

Out of the Corner of Your Eye

When we look at something, our consciousness tends to home in on whatever is at the centre of our field of vision. We pay much less attention to things on the periphery and it takes quite a lot of effort to view things in this way. When I was learning to drive, many years ago, I often had a headache by the end of each lesson. I mentioned this to a friend – someone who did not drive but was an experienced meditation teacher – and he suggested I tried keeping my eyes in a softer focus. During the next lesson everything immediately became much easier. Not only did the headaches stop, but my whole attitude to driving changed: I was now much more relaxed and even began to enjoy the process of mastering a new skill.

My friend's experience of teaching meditation had alerted him to a common problem: the tendency to confuse concentration with focusing too hard. As anyone who drives knows, fixing your eyes straight ahead is not a good strategy. It is safer to drive within a much broader picture. It's the same with meditation: if you concentrate too wilfully you will probably end up with a headache, assuming you have not already distracted yourself with something more satisfying than this regimented approach.

This is no less true of writing. If we stay too rigid – fearing to stray from the subject or the form we have chosen – we might miss something more interesting or valuable on the edge of our thoughts. So give yourself permission to break the rules. If your writing suddenly takes you in a direction that seems different to the one proposed by an exercise, go where the flow of thoughts is taking you. This is a good opportunity to learn to trust your imagination and intuition; you can always attempt the exercise again some other time. It also reminds us that in life there is usually a tension between working within existing structures and discovering new ones of our own.

To be focused is to engage the rational side of our brain, but there is another brain that seems to come into play away from the centre of our attention. This brain is more dreamlike, tending towards association and speculation, and likes to see things as other things. Try it now as you read this. What can you see to the side, out of the corner of your eye? Perhaps there is a plant to your left that could be a strange kind of bird, or a bookcase to the right that slowly takes on the form of a sky-scraper. Because you cannot be sure what these objects are, the imagi-nation gets a chance to work on them.

Another way of engaging with this wider-ranging and associative mind is to put things to one side not visually but mentally, to 'sleep on things' as the expression has it. When I was learning to play the piano I invari-ably found that if, after an intensive period of practice, I stopped play-ing for a few days, when I came back to the keyboard my fingers could do things that had previously been beyond their reach. Although I had not been practising physically, it would seem I had still been practising mentally, but with a another part of the brain. This alerts us to the fact that there are different levels of consciousness and that creative think-ing often improves when the practical part of the mind is distracted for a while.

In his novel *The End of the Affair*, Graham Greene has his main protag-onist, a writer called Maurice Bendrix, tell us:

So much in writing depends on the superficiality of one's days. One may be preoccupied with shopping and income tax returns and chance conversations, but the stream of the unconsciousness continues to flow undisturbed, solving problems, planning ahead: one sits down sterile and dispirited at the desk, and suddenly the words come as though from the air: the situations that seemed blocked in a hopeless impasse move forward: the work has been done while one slept or shopped or talked with friends.[14]

This is why many writers like to work in cafés and restaurants. It is another version of looking out of the corner of the eye: all the human activity around them preoccupies the more rational mind – which prefers the impersonal and shies away from strong feelings and original ideas – while allowing their invention free rein. There is also a greater possibility of the chance conversations that Greene refers to. It is amazing how often a stranger will provide just the right word at just the right time. Opening a book at random often produces the same effect. Among my own favourite writing places are waiting rooms at railway stations and airports, points of arrival and departure that help keep the mind more capricious and alert to fresh possibilities: finding the 'emotion' in 'motion' as the German film director Wim Wenders once described it.

Here is a poem written in a fogbound Dublin airport just before Christmas 1998:

Dublin Ghazal

The taxi's one-way radio traffic.
What are we heading for?

Did we give them a second chance,
the ones we saw most clearly?

My father stepped out of this charmed circle.
Christmas brings that home each year.

All that's left when someone dies. The empty
    spaces.
The airport filled with our own cryptic messages.

Be kind - what else is there.
Isn't that what he would have said?

The *ghazal* is a form dating back to seventh-century Arabia, and perhaps even earlier. It is a poem made up of couplets (two line stanzas) independent of each other, yet each becoming part of a whole. Traditionally, the link would have been made by the strict use of rhyme and metrical structures – although as you can see I broke these rules to enable the form to better suit my purpose. In *ghazals* – which are not narrative but associative – the meaning is not expressed or stated so much as signified. It is like a mobile with a number of different elements revolving around a central thread.

Most of the statements in this poem were observations or ideas plucked from the surrounding environment, and its form finally coalesced when I realized it was the ninth anniversary of my father's death. In many ways an airport was the perfect environment to embrace such an emotive subject – particularly Dublin with its intimations of my father's Irish ancestry. Waiting for my flight to be called I had nowhere else to go and plenty of time on my hands. As I have been suggesting, all the activity around me made it easier to mine deeper into my feelings. Surrounded by so many other people and sensory experiences, I felt less alone in the aloneness of my thoughts. Like the fact of death itself, the poem trawls for some sort of coherence out of the apparent randomness of it all.

Exercise: *Peripheral Vision*

Place a chair in the centre of a room. Just sit on it quietly for a few moments, all the while trying to relax your gaze. Become aware of your peripheral vision. Now write what you see out of the corners of your eyes in a few brief statements. These do not have to make a lot of sense; they can be quite impressionistic.

Now turn the chair through ninety degrees and repeat the process. Repeat this in ninety degree stages until the chair is back in its original position, when you should do it one more time – you will probably have a different experience from the first time.

Take each of the statements and try to condense them down to two self-contained lines. Then put these together and see if you can turn them into a poem about peripheral vision: five stanzas capturing what you saw out of the corner of your eye, your own sensibility being the central thread.

You cannot move material from one stanza to another, but you can rearrange the order of the stanzas if this creates a more interesting sequence.

This exercise is more than just about looking, it is a good way of discovering our attitude to things that are not directly in front of us, not just physically but emotionally and philosophically too: the uninvited guests of experience waiting to see if we are going to welcome them in or not.

17

Space Around the Space

The poet Michael Longley has said that in order to write poetry you need not just space, but space around the space. This is true not only of poetry but of all types of writing, and probably all types of creative thinking. Space – and its accompanying silence – unlocks the mind's riches, but such space is not easy to come by, especially in a society such as ours where we seem to have been programmed to keep ourselves busy.

Yet it does not have to be this way. Apparently the Australian Aborigines spent a good part of their waking life in 'dreamtime': the serious task of becoming trance mediums and preservers of the myths. To the Calvinistic ethic of the European colonists, this looked like anything but work. From their narrow gaze anyone sitting around doing nothing clearly had to be wasting their time. Now we have all become colonists invading our own dreamtime. Ask yourself when was the last time you sat in a chair and did absolutely nothing? I don't mean reading, or watching television, or listening to the radio, but literally doing nothing. Ironically – since it is one of the most healthy things we can do – for most of us the answer is probably when we were last feeling sick.

I sometimes get migraine headaches, and I am sure it is because I have not had enough dreamtime: time simply to muse and reflect. It has been said that depression is withheld knowledge. In like fashion I suspect my migraines are withheld stillness, my whole being screaming for me to stop doing and just be. I always feel much better after I have had a migraine! As our lives become busier, this just being is a very difficult thing to achieve. For one thing, it is probably too close for comfort by reminding us that little of what we do is really *that* important, certainly not important enough to get stressed out about it. Because of this compulsion to be active, if stillness is going to be possible it needs to be held within some sort of framework. Meditation is a very good place to start.

Sitting in a chair and doing nothing may be beyond your reach. But sitting in the same chair and following your breath is immediately more graspable. Drawing the breath in then letting it go provides enough activity to hold the awareness without being over-stimulating. Using the breath in this way is in fact the basis of one of the commonest forms of meditation, called the 'mindfulness of breathing'. This is usually done in four stages and gradually guides you from broad awareness to something more focused.[15] To give you a sense of it, try the following exercise:

Exercise: *Following the Breath*

Write at the top of a page in your notebook the word 'IN', and on the next page the word 'OUT'.

Sit quietly on a chair in an upright posture with your feet flat on the floor. Close your eyes and take a few deep breaths, feeling your body relax as you breathe out. Then let the breath become more natural, fast or slow, shallow or deep, whatever feels right. Gradually, with each in-breath, gently say to yourself, 'in', and do this for about five minutes. If you find your mind wandering, be patient with yourself; just bring yourself back to the next breath which will be there waiting for you.

Slowly open your eyes and under the word 'IN' in your notebook write the following statement: 'The breath comes in.'

Breathe in and out, and write another statement, replacing the word 'breath' with whatever word or words come to mind, for example, 'The sea comes in.' Repeat this process for about five minutes. It doesn't matter how long it takes you to write each statement, but be sure to take a complete breath between one statement and the next. If you get stuck trying to think of a new word, just repeat the last statement.

Put your notebook down and return to simply following your breath, if necessary preparing yourself as before. This time, however, say 'out' gently to yourself with each out breath, and again do this for about five minutes.

Then repeat the writing exercise but now replace the word 'breath' in the statement 'The breath goes out.'

It is such a simple thing to notice you are breathing, and yet so profound, the whole of life being enacted in a single moment, since, in the same way that each breath comes and goes, so do we absorb new events and relinquish old ones.

Even doing an awareness of the breath practice for five minutes – especially if it is every day – will have a positive effect. It will bring some well-deserved peace and calm into your life, and also give you a taste of doing nothing, or at least not being so busy. It builds a spaciousness into our experience which (as you may have discovered in the exercise) can then be translated into our writing practice. In a world hell-bent on activity, these moments as we follow the breath – or as we wait, pen motionless in hand, for the next idea to arise – provide an invaluable form of 'dream-catcher'. They are 'space around the space', here and now in the present moment.

18

Learning to Read

Exercise: *Revising*

Take a piece of your own writing – a short poem or a prose extract – and each day, for seven days, try to rewrite it. At the beginning of each new session go back to the original and start again. Keep all your drafts, numbering them sequentially each day, but do not refer to them from one day to the next. At the end of the week read through all the different drafts and select the version you think best. Then trace the route that led you towards it, or led you away from it. Apart from anything else, this exercise is a reminder to keep all your drafts until you are sure something is absolutely finished. Hidden within them may be a jewel that is only revealed on a subsequent reading. Sometimes time will have been the best editor.

A good writer must also be a good reader. James Joyce once spent a whole day working on two sentences in *Ulysses* – not on which words to use – he had already decided that – but simply on their order. So what would you have made of this?

Perfume of embraces all him assailed. With hungered flesh obscurely, he mutely craved to adore.[16]

Fifteen words in a novel over 900 pages long. It is the moment in which the main character, Leopold Bloom, muses on his wife's sensuality as he is walking down a Dublin street. None of the words is particularly unusual, but Joyce felt it worth shuffling them until they achieved just the right mixture of erotic wonder. To do this he had to be a careful reader – reading not just with the eye but also with the ear – to be sure he struck precisely the right tone of voice to convey Bloom's inner world.

It is not only great literary figures like Joyce who are touched by this search for perfection. Here is the opening sentence of Ian Fleming's first James Bond novel, *Casino Royale*:

> *Scent and smoke hit the taste buds with an acid thwack at three o'clock in the morning.*

Nothing wrong with that you might think. It pitches us straight in there with the right degree of physicality. Except this was not his opening sentence, only his first attempt at it. He then rewrote it as:

> *Scent and smoke and sweat can suddenly combine together and hit the taste buds with an acid shock at three o'clock in the morning.*

This has gained some 'sweat' with its connotations of nervousness, exertion, and excitement; but perhaps it has lost some verve in the process. That is OK though, because sometimes you have to give yourself the freedom to get worse before you can get better. It seems Fleming felt the same way, since the final published version was:

> The scent and smoke and sweat of a casino are nauseating at three in
> the morning.[17]

This has the tautness of the first version combined with the acidity of
the second. The masterstroke was to add 'casino'. Not only does this as-
sonate with the sounds of 'scent' and 'smoke', it also tells us exactly
where we are, which is no mean feat at three in the morning. It provides
an air of authenticity that the other versions lack, although they only
lack them in retrospect because Fleming had taken the trouble to read
them to himself so carefully.

'Who cares?' you might ask. It is just the opening of a James Bond
thriller, to be read and then put down again. But Fleming obviously
cared: cared enough to work his material until it said exactly what he
wanted it to convey. He did this because, like Joyce, he understood that
each experience is unique, and the more accurately it is captured, the
more it solicits the reader's capacity for identification. Bond has sur-
vived where other fictional spies have come and gone because the
books are so well written. They have lasting value because they last in
the mind.

If James Bond and Leopold Bloom are worthy of such attention, are not
you and I? Spending time editing our work – maybe more time than it
took us to write it – requires us to start taking it much more seriously.
And this asks us not only to trust the richness of our imagination, but
also the details of experience that feed it; perfect, after all, means complete or whole. Careful editing is a way of noting what William Blake
called the minute particulars, reminding us of the intrinsic relationship
between the things we perceive and the way we perceive them. Our
world is ultimately 'mind created', owing its origins to ideas in the
mind.

There is another aspect of this rereading and rewriting process that is worth stating: if we begin editing something, we had better know when to stop. How often do we undo the good already done by going one step too far? Think of the cake left in the oven a moment too long, the words of support that stray fatally into advice, the extra session of meditation that becomes a practice of wilfulness instead of mindfulness. This means refining our judgements so that we are eventually able to recognize the rightness of something as soon as we chance upon it.

But where does such a sense come from? It is partly a matter of trial and error: learning from your mistakes and trying your writing out on other people – particularly other writers – to see if they pick up on the same things as you do. There is also the communion with writers created in our mind when we read their work, for good writers encourage good reading. Perhaps this is what we mean by their style: showing us ways to extend and enrich language that would never have occurred to us on our own.

You can take this a stage further and explicitly model something you write on an existing work – learning how the masters do it by trying the same things yourself. This is, after all, the way great artists of the past learned their craft. And if what you produce seems to be only a pale imitation, that's alright because this is only meant to be an exercise. If the original piece of writing touches off something important to you, the differences in your preoccupations and circumstances will eventually take over.

Another useful editing tip comes from the Russian poet Joseph Brodsky. He suggested that when you have finished a piece of writing always go back to see if you really need the first thing you wrote – the first paragraph of a piece of prose, or the first lines or stanza of a poem. This opening flourish is often just a preliminary stage – akin to talking to yourself – to get you into the subject, and not really necessary to the work as a whole. One of the values of Brodsky's observation is that it reminds us that the writing process and the reading process are not the same thing.

It is true that Allen Ginsberg famously said, 'first thought, best thought,' and sometimes this will prove to be absolutely correct. Perhaps the initial impulse that prompted you to write was so pure, so raw, that you will never be able to recapture it; one certainly feels this with a lot of Ginsberg's poems. But, in my experience, it will often take steady and repeated effort to get to your 'best thought'. So don't despair of all those drafts piling up before you as you write. Instead, welcome them as other versions of yourself: work in progress that will, with careful reading, contribute to that elusive perfect paragraph or stanza.

19

Not Just Saying, But Saying Well

Although it is useful to remind ourselves that if we cannot write we should lower our standards, this does not mean that standards in themselves are a bad thing; the issue is knowing when and where to apply them. At the moment of creation, trying to evade the inner critic is a very shrewd move, because, if we learn to accept our bad ideas, better ones may follow in their wake. But at the level of publishing or performing, standards are vital. Remember it is not necessary for everything we write to be inflicted on the rest of the world. Some pieces are best seen as experiments: invaluable as part of an ongoing process but without much shelf-life.

We need to make a distinction between expression and articulation. Everybody has feelings, and feelings are usually best expressed, which is one of the main values of the exercises in this book. But for writing to become art requires not just saying, but saying well. It is not just a matter of expression, but also of articulation within a specific medium and the discipline of a craft. Ultimately, the artist seeks to address issues that – for them at least – can *only* be addressed in their chosen way, whether in a poem, a novel, or a play.

If this is not understood, undue distress can occur when a piece of writing – whose prime concern is self-expression – is later dismissed in a context – such as submission for publication or a competition – where more traditional literary values prevail. These values inevitably mean making comparisons with writers whose work has already been recognized. Although most of us will come off second-best in these comparisons, this should be a cause for celebration, not alarm. All those names on the bookshelves show us what has already been achieved and what may yet be possible. We can learn from others' mistakes and build on their successes.

The idea of hierarchy – that maybe someone *is* better at something than someone else – is not such a comfortable one for us these days. Instead, our culture places a lot of emphasis on autonomy and authenticity, urging us all to become our own masters. Nevertheless, because the arts work through pleasures of the senses, they might provide a way of re-awakening our *sense* of standards without it feeling like a religious sermon. If you find writers you like, you quite naturally want to read more of them, and since it is the quality of their writing that makes them so readable – and rereadable – whether you think in these terms or not, in all but name you will be attending their master classes.

Although it is understandable that we feel despair when we compare our 'feeble' efforts to those of the great writers who have gone before us, I suggest you acknowledge these feelings, but then try to put them to one side. The Argentinian writer Jorge Luis Borges said that geniuses create their precursors. In other words, we often see the worth of some-one's writing only in retrospect. This is another version of the teaching of conditionality: that things arise within a matrix of relationships. Who is to say how your writing might eventually influence other peo-ple? One day some future master may even be depending upon you. So keep reading other people's work, and keep writing your own.

Exercise: *Influences*

Think of a writer you particularly like and write about how you are connected to their 'lineage' by answering the follow-ing questions:

(1) Historically: Why, where, and when did you first read their work? Was it on the recommendation of a family member, teacher, or friend? Or was it prompted by something you saw in the media or a chance encounter in a bookshop or library? Or was it through another writer they were influenced by, or who influenced them?

(2) Existentially: Was there something in their writing that addressed philosophical or spiritual issues that were, or subsequently became, vitally important to you?

(3) Mythically: In what way do you feel this writer speaks to you alone? How do they touch your deepest hopes and fears, your 'fate'?

20

Every Word Counts

Writers have a love affair with words. They rejoice that there are so many ways of saying the same thing – or nearly the same thing, because each minute shift in vocabulary will subtly change the meaning and the tone. Take the word 'rejoice' that I just used. I could easily have chosen 'celebrate' as an alternative verb. So:

> *They rejoice that there are so many ways of saying the same thing.*

becomes:

> *They celebrate that there are so many ways of saying the same thing.*

There is not much difference in the meaning, but if you read it out loud you will hear there has been a shift in the sound. In the original sentence the soft 'c' of 'rejoice' prepares us for the 's' sounds that follow: 'so', 'ways', 'saying' and 'same'. To a lesser extent, there is a faint echo of the 'o' between 'rejoice' and 'so', but can you hear the immediate impact – like a faint clash of cymbals – that the hard 't' sound of 'celebrate' makes with the last 't' of 'that' in the new version? Now there is a slight aural climax before the sentence continues.

'So what?' you might be thinking. Well believe me, this is the kind of thing that writers lose sleep over. It is the equivalent of wondering whether to paint the walls of your home pink, brown, or yellow. It will always be the same place in terms of size and space, but the colours will make a huge difference to whether you want to live there or not. Nowhere is this sensitivity to the power of words more acute than in poetry, in particular within the minimal resources of the haiku. Here, for example, is a marvellous modern haiku by the Irish poet Seamus Heaney:

1.I.87

Dangerous pavements.
But I face the ice this year
With my father's stick.[18]

Notice how much Heaney achieves in just three lines, and thirteen words – which add up (in the pattern 5–7–5) to the seventeen syllables to which the haiku limits itself. Is his father dead? We don't know, and perhaps it doesn't matter. What we do know is that the narrator is at an age where he needs support to 'face the ice'. Within the poem's snap-shot, we sense that time is catching up on him. And listen to how the mellifluous (and thus slippery) first line gives way to the gentle tapping of the next two lines – the steady beat of the stick repeated in the sound of all those one-syllable words.

Just as subtle is the suggestion of transience, contingency, and bereave-ment, conveyed by the image of a walking-stick passed from father to son. This reminds us that the haiku was originally a Japanese form – set in the present moment and located in a specific season of the year – designed to carry three ideas about things in the natural world: that they are transient, they are contingent, and, if we fail to admit this, they will eventually bring suffering.

These are ideas at the core of Buddhist metaphysics, since the haiku emerged from the practice of Zen Buddhism. But the haiku does not lecture us on these things, just as Heaney's poem does not advertise its pedigree, although the sum of its title $(1+1+8+7)$ is exactly the number of syllables used in the traditional haiku. Instead, using one or two key images with both spontaneity and absolute clarity – like the few lines of ink used to create a landscape in Japanese and Chinese painting – the haiku places these teachings in our mind's eye and our heart's ear.

Therefore when a traditional haiku poet talks about falling blossom, or a mountain disappearing in mist, these are a direct apprehension of the philosophical truth of cause and effect, or, as it is known in Buddhism, conditionality. But conditionality, being dry and technical, can leave us unmoved, whereas Heaney's haiku, for example, despite its chilly locale, leaves us with a feeling of warmth and gladness. He is reminding us that within the winds of time and decay we must stand firm, passing love and wisdom ever onwards from one generation to the next. Heaney, making no claim to be a Buddhist, reminds us that the Buddha's insights into impermanence are a matter not of religious conviction but of human observation.

When in every other sphere of life language is in constant danger of being devalued – underplayed yet oversold – it is the writer's task to keep our sensitivity to the way we communicate alive. Surrounded by sound bites and screaming headlines, technical jargon and advertising clichés, we need the quiet sensitivity of poets like Seamus Heaney to remind us of the depths of which that language is actually capable. This is a sensitivity that helps us to refine the dialogue we conduct both between and within ourselves, making us better able to recognize the dichotomy between what we mean and what we say, and consequently between what we really feel and what we would like to feel.

Matsuo Basho, the great seventeenth-century Japanese poet, said that the function of the haiku is to 'rectify common speech'. In marked contrast to the deceptiveness of sound bites and the exclusivity of jargon, it asks us to keep language clear and straightforward. At the same time, limiting its resources means that every word has to count. Although it is true that jargon and sound bites also count words, they do so in a miserly fashion, aiming not for inclusiveness and lucidity but to exclude by giving as little away as possible.

Modern means of communication are paraded to look like an efficient use of language, when in fact they display laziness, even disdain, masked to look like efficiency. The really efficient language is poetry – and none more so than the haiku – where every word is made to glance in a host of different ways so as to capture as many associations as possible. This is why poetry is sometimes puzzling on its first reading but full of insight at the more intuitive level, below the surface texture. Poets remember that each and every word was once awesome in its magical power to reproduce a wisp or whisper of the world, before, that is, it got blunted by familiarity.

Exercise: *Haiku*

Using Seamus Heaney's '1.1.87' as a model, write a short poem that celebrates your relationship with a friend or member of your family. Let the poem be guided primarily by your feelings. It is the spirit of the haiku we are after, rather than an exact replica of its form, so it is enough to aim for a poem of three lines: a short one, a long one, and a short one; though if you want to be more strict you can also follow the syllable count of 5+7+5.

Write in the present tense, keeping the language as simple as possible. And build the poem around one clear image, just as

Heaney used the walking-stick. Aim to 'show' your emotions rather than 'tell' them, in order to convey, like Heaney, the inner world through items – pavements, ice, a walking-stick – drawn from daily life. You do not need to mention a particular season, but restrict the poem to the present and to one location.

If you find this difficult, keep coming back to it. Remember the task we are setting ourselves when we write in poetic forms is nothing less than that of transforming the way we shape our thoughts.

21

Writing Like You Talk

Whether we explain it by chance, our early conditioning, or the fruits of previous karma, it is undoubtedly true that some of us will have more innate ability as writers than others. Similarly, some people make better teachers or better carpenters. Whatever our talent, there is one thing in which we can always excel during a writing exercise: being ourselves. No one can do this better than we can; indeed, we are the *only* person who can do this. In particular that means – perhaps for the first time in our lives – trusting the value of our own voice, our unique way of expressing things. Only then should we be concerned whether other people will be interested in what we have to say.

At least to begin with, do not worry about the literary quality of what you write. Instead do as Natalie Goldberg suggests: 'Simply write like you talk, nothing fancy.' I know this works because I tried it with my mother. Over the phone she told me a story about a visit to Lundy – an island off the coast of north Devon where she lives, and famous for its puffins. I was so moved by her story that I asked her to write it out for me, but she declined, making the usual excuses: 'I'm no writer, I have terrible handwriting,' etc. etc. So I played a trick on her: 'But that's the point: I want to use your writing in a workshop, to show that anyone can do it, even a eighty-year-old grandmother. All you have to do is write out what you just told me. If it helps, think of it as a letter.' I suppose she thought I meant to hold up her story as an example of a 'bad' piece of writing, but of course, as I hope you realize by now, in the workshop context there is no bad writing. I was trying to get her to lower her standards.

The last 'creative' writing my mother did was at school in London – she still talks with a Cockney accent. As a girl she won a poetry prize. This reminds me of something William Stafford said when asked when he first became a poet. He replied, 'That's the wrong question. You should ask everyone else when they stopped.' There is still, I am sure, a poet in my mother, as I am sure there is a poet in all of us, if this means a need to experience the world in a more enchanted way through the charmed play of language. So I am glad that I encouraged my mother to trust the 'poet' in her at least one more time. This is her story, written out much as she spoke it.

We thought the day was ideal for the crossing from Bideford: clear sky, and little wind. One-and-a-half hours on, when we arrived at Lundy, the captain of the Oldenburg said it was one of the worst crossings this year. I certainly found my sea-legs. Sue and I decided to walk the first side of the island before lunch. We walked for about two miles and never saw one person; guess they were in the 'tavern'. It was so peaceful, I could not put into a few words about all the beauty around us. All the birds were in full song, almost as though they knew we were around. We saw lots of rabbits, deer, goats, and horses. Also managed to spot a couple of seals going from sea to rocks. But not one puffin to be seen.

We reached the furthest point of the left side of the island and it looked as though the sky was touching the sea, because we were so high up on the rocks above the sea. We started to make our way back to the small village, where we had started from. On a different path back we came to a field, and there eating grass was a large horse. Near the fence was a smaller horse. I have a habit of talking to all the cats and dogs I meet, so why not this horse? While I was saying, you are beautiful, what's your name, I froze. Her eyes looked straight into mine, no sign of her being afraid of me, almost as if we had met before. Sue came back after looking for other animals and said, 'What is the matter with you?' I said that horse would talk if it could. Sue looked down and said, look that is the reason, her leg is bleeding and two bones are sticking out. We ran a long way before we came to a repair shed with a man working in it. I said please get that horse to a vet. He was so grateful we had made the effort to find someone.

The horse had to be shot. I went mad at the man when he told us. I said why? I had seen on a television vet programme that they mend horses legs, but he said they could not mend the leg, it was broken too badly. I was sorry I never found out her name, but I will call her Lundy. I will always wonder why it had such a strange effect on me.

We walked back the other side of the island in the afternoon. Then another surprise. Near the old lighthouse there were dozens of rabbits, all different colours. It was so unusual to see some that were jet black. They did not seem to worry about us, while having a great time. A few skylarks sent us on our way. Soon it will be off home again. It will be a day I will never forget.

Exercise: ***Capturing the Way You Talk***

The idea of this exercise is to try to capture the way you talk; so ideally you would record yourself and then play it back and transcribe exactly what you hear. If you can't do this, speak aloud and write what you say a sentence at a time. (You could of course get a friend to do the transcribing for you.)

The subject is a personal story: perhaps a tale of holidays, of childhood, of calamities, or of love. The subject matter is not as important as the way you tell it: just you telling your story – one detail at a time – in as natural a voice as possible.

22

Walking

People Who Come Here

People who come here say 'wind in the pines'.
Their pens whisper and scratch.
'Skin of the loch', they write.
The loch scuds, or stares.

At night the trees press the ghosts of their ears
to the windows, to hear their names
passed like a pipe in a circle.

The lochs who come here form people on banks
muttering 'stones on the mountain'. The people
paste tiny white flags in their cave
saying 'paper on stone'.
The stones weep, or wait.[19]

This poem, about the osmosis between human beings and their surroundings, was written by Julia Lewis during a writing workshop at Dhanakosa, a Buddhist retreat centre on the shore of Loch Voil in the highlands of Scotland. The locals say it is a 'thin' place where the fairy world meets our own. It certainly has a magical atmosphere, which Julia has captured in her poem. The waters of Loch Voil are often so still and opaque – particularly during the summer when this workshop took place – that they become a mirror. In the same way Julia's poem reflects, via its mysterious and mischievous catalogue, the experience of being a writer out in the natural world.

Much of the time, though, we are not so reflective about our environment. We do not give it much attention, either because it is so harsh and unattractive that all we want to do is try to ignore it, or because we have seen it so many times before that we start to take it for granted. So we need to find ways to cleanse and reawaken the senses. Sometimes we can do this by going somewhere completely new – particularly if, like Loch Voil, it is a place of incredible natural beauty. We can also see things afresh through the lens of the arts since, as Julia's poem shows, the aesthetic experience sharpens and focuses our awareness. But although we expect to see painters and photographers working in nature, writing today seems to have retreated inside and become ever more desk-bound.

It was not always like this. The Chinese and Japanese Zen Buddhist poets celebrated nature and the natural life by living quietly in mountain hermitages. Nearer to home, Wordsworth was famous for composing his poems as he walked back and forth in his garden, on level ground so that he could keep the metre; whereas his friend Coleridge found he needed to walk up and down the steep hills of Somerset.

Taking this as an example, walking is the basis of the following exercise, which entices us to write in and about our environment by the use of a simple ritual. The physical act itself might be completely familiar, but by applying some unfamiliar restraints we are compelled to experience both walking and the landscape it leads us through in a new way.

Exercise: *Writing and Walking*

Take a walk of exactly one thousand steps. Stop every one hundred steps and write about your experience of walking, such as the thoughts and feelings that have arisen, and/or what you now see and hear in your immediate surroundings.

I must admit that when we first devised this exercise I was not sure that a thousand steps would be enough. But having tried it – as it happens, in the car park of the Buddhist business, Windhorse:evolution, where Ananda and I were exploring the idea of creativity in the workplace – I was amazed how much happened and how far the walk had taken me. A thousand steps was much further than I had expected, particularly when I had given each step so much of my attention.

This is an idea explored by the Scottish poet, Thomas A. Clark, in his prose poem, 'In Praise of Walking', when he notices:

> That something exists outside ourselves and our preoccupations, so near, so readily available, is our greatest blessing.

And, a little later,

> The pace of a walk will determine the number and variety of things to be encountered, from the broad outlines of a mountain range to a tit's nest among the lichen, and the quality of attention that will be brought to bear upon them.[20]

Walking 'mindfully' reminds us how rich the world that surrounds us actually is. And, as Clark suggests, the slower our pace, the more there is to see. Even a gravel path beside a car park holds an infinity of textures and an infinite number of responses. At least for a moment, an encounter has grown into a relationship, since to know something in this detail is inevitably to begin to care about it. This is why we should try this exercise in our immediate environment. We need to be re-minded that we share a mutual dependence. Would we, for example, casually throw litter if we took the time to see where it landed?

When places have become dull, we have to make them fascinating again. As writers, we should aim to invest our town or city with the same exoticness that someone who has never been there before would give it. The ordinary and the extraordinary: only a short prefix distin-guishes them, but the time it takes to see the difference changes our world.

23

Monologues

I used to know someone who was unrelentingly talkative, but at least he was honest about it. He once said to me, 'Basically, I talk to myself. Occasionally someone else interrupts and calls it conversation.' The next exercise gives you permission to keep talking without fear of interruption, because it is in the form of a monologue. This time, though, the challenge is not to write the way *you* talk, but the way someone else does. Here is a good example that one of our students, Valerie Witonska, wrote on a recent workshop, this one being in the form of a poem, but it doesn't have to be.

Gertie Contemplates Dhanakosa

Last week I goes on this writing wotsit,
retreat they calls it.
I wondered if it would be a bit
la-di-da, but it wasn't.

There was these two fellas
with funny names
but they turned up trumps,
made us feel very comfy.

I was gobsmacked at
what came out of my mouth.
You'd call it filth I dare say,
but they took it all in good part.

People wrote some lovely stuff about
kids playing with stones, red squirrels,
Indian slums, shopping in Lewisham,
and this creepy one about being killed by a lily.

They did this thing called meditation
where you sit very still for a long time:
sometimes you shift about a bit
but sometimes you feel tingly and calm all over.

In my dorm four of us was sharing.
Two of us roaring snorers
but we had this stuff called
Snoring Stop you had to gargle with.

We did it to the tune of
'Come on Baby do the Locomotion'.
I laughed so much I could have wet myself
If I hadn't just been.

We was in this lovely place
called Danny something.
And there was this big lake
what Scottish call a loch.

This loch is huge
with high hills round it
all green they was
with grass and loads of trees.

It's sort of quiet
like your heart has found its home.
You want to never leave it; plunge right in,
though it was bitter freezing when I did.[21]

The interesting thing about this is that, although it is not the way the poet actually speaks, it could be; by which I mean not that Gertie *is* Val but that you can hear echoes of Val in the things Gertie says. Gertie is like Val's secret sister, her alter ego, who shadows her and is never seen, but is sometimes heard in her writing. That is why this piece works so well. It has the air of both authenticity and sly revelation. It is a chance for Val to try something out. I suggest you do the same by writing your monologue in the voice of a character – perhaps someone you know, someone you have invented, or another version of yourself that you do not usually reveal. Welcome them with open arms, trying to see them as honestly as you can, unbiased by your conventional responses. Remember they may like things that you cannot abide, and say things you would never dream of saying. As Gertie (or is it also Val) tells us, 'I was gobsmacked at what come out of my mouth.'

Before you start writing there are a few questions to be asked in order to help your character to talk. First, and most obviously, who is the speaker? If you don't know, it's going to be very difficult to maintain an authentic voice throughout – you could start speaking as one person but end up sounding like another.

Secondly, whom is the speaker addressing? If you think about it, the people we are talking to go a long way to defining what we say. It may be a soliloquy of course, like Hamlet's, but even then you are talking to someone; it just happens to be yourself. And this could be very significant because, as the novelist Geoffrey Household observes, it is relatively easy for a man to confess the lies he tells himself, but much harder for him to confess the truth he tells himself.

The third thing to clarify is where and when the monologue takes place. It is one of the strengths of Val's piece that even if you have never been to a writing workshop (a 'wotsit') such as Wolf at the Door, or a Buddhist retreat centre such as Dhanakosa ('Danny something'), you would still get a strong sense of these from what Gertie says. Of course, it is her own cheeky take on it, but because Gertie is so well defined the things she talks about also assume an objective reality.

Finally, ask yourself what is happening? A speech at a wedding is not going to be the same as one delivered at a funeral. If you do not know what is going on, it is hardly reasonable to expect someone else to know. This touches on one of the most important lessons of this exercise and writing generally: the ability to put yourself in someone else's shoes: not just your character's shoes but your reader's as well. Remember that when you write something you have a whole world of associations stacking up behind the things you say. These associations will be the result of your own unique experiences and your memories of them. You must therefore ask yourself whether the reader is able to make sense of what you write – bring to life, their own life – without access to this private world?

Writing a monologue is an opportunity to step from one reality into another. Paradoxically, the demands of finding the accurate social and psychological details that will make a character seem convincing – in the way that Val made Gertie authentic – inevitably force us back on our own experience. This means that if we say out loud what our character is saying (as I strongly recommend you do) we in effect become our own audience. This is what Alan Bennett, a modern master of the monologue, was alluding to when he observed that it is in the process of imitating other people's voices that we come to better understand the sound of our own. Possibly for the first time we have consciously set up something against which to measure the way we express ourselves. It is talking like a ventriloquist, by learning to listen with your mouth. In writing a monologue all those ghostly conversations we have with ourselves in our own mind are suddenly brought to life.

24

An Ever-Widening Circle

Many of the exercises used in this book are adapted from Wolf at the Door writing workshops. What would you see at one of these events? First, a group of people sitting in a circle. Between Ananda and me is the listening chair I have already described, waiting for someone to step forward and read: those remarkable moments when we are presented with another person's emotional and intellectual reality. Probably the most distinctive feature of the workshop, however, is the concentrated silence as people work at their writing. Because concentration tends to be contagious it is a silence that helps nurture our creativity. Even if writing will ultimately be a solitary act – in a room of other people you will still be alone with your thoughts – just the sight of someone else's moving pen can be enough to keep yours moving too.

Furthermore, other people open up possibilities that might never have occurred to you by yourself. They may be better readers of your work than you are, and spot things, good and bad, that you had failed to notice. They can even see success when you are still haunted by doubt or fear of failure. So I would strongly encourage you to get together with other writers from time to time.

If you cannot find a writers' group nearby, why not start something yourself? It doesn't take much effort. You could meet in your living-room or at a local café. Ideally it should be for people you already know and feel comfortable with – and certainly a group of people you want to get to know better, since that is going to happen whether you like it or not. You can set topics to write about (the exercises in this book will give you a start) and bring the results along to each meeting. It doesn't matter whether you combine people who are primarily interested in poetry, drama, and fiction, or even letter-writing, journals, and other types of non-fiction. Having such a mix helps to keep things fresh, and the different categories can occasionally separate out once things start to develop.

I would, however, suggest a few ground rules. Even if you decide not to use a 'listening chair', I would recommend you keep to the principle that when someone is reading no one is to interrupt them; it is hard enough to read aloud as it is. For the same reason it should always be acceptable for people to share their work without comments necessarily being made afterwards. And make sure the group does not simply become an opportunity to deride or discount other people's work – or, even more importantly, the experiences and emotions that lie behind it. Regardless of whether you are a Buddhist, the ideal of 'perfect speech' will provide a useful framework to set the guidelines, specifically: truthful communication, kindly communication, meaningful communication, and harmonious communication. Or to put these negatively, since these are the warning signals you should be looking out for: false speech, harsh speech, frivolous speech, and slanderous speech.

If, as the group becomes more confident, you decide to attempt more detailed readings of each other's work, you could try using the method that Ananda and I have adapted from the critic and teacher Philip Hobsbaum: the writers read their work but make no comment until the end of the discussion. The other people say what they think the writing is about, all the things they like about it, and finally the areas where they think it needs more work. Only when these stages are complete is the writer allowed to respond. If there are no other writers around you,

you could still use this method with a group of people long-distance, transmitting work and feedback by email or by letter.

By the end of these workshops a wonderful sense of intimacy will have developed, one of the measures of this being that things people have read stay with you, cropping up months later in dreams, meditations, and in your own writing. In this sense the circle of the workshop is not static but an ever-widening circle. And it holds hallowed ground for, in the words of W.B. Yeats,

> I have spread my dreams under your feet;
> Tread softly because you tread on my dreams.[22]

25

Rules and Rituals

I once read an interview with a novelist who explained that before she began each day's writing she would leave her house to go for a walk round the block, and only then enter her study. She called this her 'walk to work'. Although it sounds eccentric, this little rite holds a lot of wisdom. It puts a gap between everyday activity and the intensity of writing. In effect, she was reminding herself that her writing room was a ritual space, a place where normal rules do not apply. For the same reason, it is customary to remove your shoes when you enter a meditation hall. In this ritual space she could spend ten minutes, or even an hour, staring out of the window pondering on what the next word should be, and know that this was *not* a waste of time.

Writing is an activity in which rules can start to become practices. Take the idea of imposing a ten-minute time limit on most of the exercises in this book. It is true that this puts pressure on you to keep the pen moving, which might be construed as a limitation. But it is also true that keeping the pen moving offers a chance for liberation by staying one step ahead of the inner critic. Now you are learning to lower your standards, allowing yourself the freedom to attempt something without worrying if it doesn't turn out perfect, at least not immediately.

I have also suggested that if you have a good idea that leads you away from the apparent goal, then follow the golden thread of your thinking, since you can try the exercise again another time. This is, however, only a rule of thumb. You might be someone who is temperamentally prone to distraction, forever hankering after the next sensation. This being the case it will be wiser to stick to the exercise and not feed your monkey mind – as they call it in Zen – too many fresh bananas.

Is there a good time to write? A good place? Well I can tell you what works for me, but it is best to experiment and see what works for you. Perhaps you are a social 'day person' whereas I am a solitary 'night person', meaning these are the conditions under which your mind is going to be most alert and imaginative. If you don't know the most fruitful time and place for writing, find out by trial and error. Do the same exercise at different times and places – the ten-minute timed writing would be a good one to choose since it is so untrammelled – and compare results.

Remember that the aim is to establish positive routines in which rules become rituals. For example, if I don't meditate first thing in the morning there is a very good chance I will not do it at all that day. And a day without meditation feels to me like a wasted opportunity to bring some 'sense' into my life: a deeper sense of who I am and who I might yet be. If you have a similar tendency in writing it is best to be honest about it. Schedule a regular time and try to stick to it.

It is clearly up to you whether you attempt to get your work published – but bear in mind there are standard guidelines for submissions, such as always including a self-addressed stamped envelope, and not sending too much material: half a dozen poems, two or three stories, or one chapter from a novel is enough. Although you cannot predict the outcome, at least ensure that your work is legible by presenting a clean and tidy manuscript. Editors are busy people – and many magazines and presses are run for love rather than money – so do what you can to help their cause.

I must admit that when I conceived this book I never saw it in terms of how to write prize-winning poems or best-selling stories and novels. But I am confident it presents a firm foundation for such things, because (as Ananda says of our workshops) its main purpose is to kick-start the imagination. I certainly think it's a good idea to test your writing in the world, which for some may mean no more than joining a writing workshop or reading group as described in Chapter 24.

If you do try to publish, don't be impatient for success. Otherwise one of two things can happen: either you'll get rejected and lose heart, or you'll get accepted and lose your open-heartedness: you could be tempted to stay with what you know and just write to a formula. It may even be a prize-winning formula, but what have you won if your vision is lost in the process? There is also a danger that you will be writing simply to keep getting approval, whereas approval is something we should strive to give ourselves. First and foremost, the art of writing – certainly from the spiritual perspective I have been exploring – is about how to awaken freedom, wisdom, and compassion, and then, as a natural human response, the desire to share these qualities with other people.

26

Excuses

The question is not whether we are creative – I hope the writing exercises have convinced you of this by now – but whether we allow ourselves to be creative. We have imbibed so many strategies to block ourselves; we have spent a lifetime accumulating excuses.

Exercise: **Excuses**

Make a list of excuses for your inability to write.

I cannot write because . . . . . .

The best response to this I have heard is, 'I cannot write because I am too busy making a sign for my door which says, "Writing, Do Not Disturb".' This raises the question of which side of the door the sign should be displayed on, because all too often, alas, it is ourselves, not other people, who disturb our writing. It is amazing how, as soon as we pick up the pen or turn on the computer, all the things we had forgotten to do, or forgotten we wanted to do, come flooding back. I have yet to meet a writer who has not experienced this at some time or another. It is not whether we have excuses, but how best we can respond to them.

The Buddhist teachings about the hindrances to meditation might provide some clues. Traditionally there are said to be five hindrances: hatred or ill will, desire for sense experience, restlessness and anxiety, sloth and torpor, and doubt and indecision. At any given time, one of these will usually be dominant. It might be restlessness and anxiety that comes to the fore. If we also feel a sudden sense of aversion to the task in hand, or the desire to be distracted by the things around us, or we have an inexplicable sense of tiredness, or we persistently question the value of what we are doing, these may mask the underlying sense of unease about where this particular meditation or piece of writing is demanding that we go.

Simply recognizing the presence of the distraction is often sufficient to keep it within manageable proportions. Now we are no longer under the power of confusion, but have begun to assert our individuality on what we are trying to do. If this does not work, there are a number of tried and tested methods for overcoming the hindrances. I have used all of them at one time or another, and they do seem to work in both meditation and writing.

We can try adopting what is traditionally described as a sky-like attitude, which is to say recognizing that everything is transient – like clouds in the sky – including our current state of mind. Thus we could reflect on a time when we did feel inspired to write and see if we can transfer some of these feelings into the present. If nothing else, this approach will hopefully make it easier to feel less stuck. Or we can consider the consequences of persisting with the distraction – for example, a golden opportunity will have been lost. Another suggestion is to try to cultivate the opposite state, for example to replace feelings of agitation with a sense of calm. One way to support this would be to write for one minute, pause for a moment, and then write for two minutes before pausing again, and slowly build up the writing time so as to acknowledge the hindrance without being overwhelmed by it. A related method is to begin training ourselves to deliberately put the distraction to one side, which is clearly the philosophy behind timed writings.

Finally, there is what in fact is the most fundamental and far-reaching approach, traditionally called 'going for refuge' – a technical Buddhist term which, put simply, means asking yourself what it is that you are *really* committed to. All writers should ask themselves this question from time to time, for there is no shame in admitting that your interests lie elsewhere.

Of course we can add another method for overcoming the hindrances, and that is lowering our standards. In particular this can help to deal with restlessness and anxiety and ill will towards ourselves – the sense that there is no room for us to make mistakes. As I have already pointed out, there is no better place to start working with this lack of self-esteem than in our writing. Writing can be a rehearsal, not a final per-formance – a rehearsal for our love, for our grief, for our success, for our failure; the stage being the present moment and our own mind. It is not just the things we do on this stage, but also the things we do not do – the excuses we make for not being able to write – that tell us a great deal about ourselves. An empty page is not necessarily the same thing as an empty mind.

27

A Wolf in Sheep's Clothing

The first time I went on a Buddhist retreat – a few days in peaceful surroundings, away from our usual concerns and routines – we were told that we should be careful when we went back into the world because we might be more open and sensitive than we realized. It was good advice: practices such as meditation and devotional rituals can subtly increase our awareness, allowing us to drop the defences we have spent a lifetime building up. Having begun to tune in to ourselves more deeply, the sudden onslaught of the harsh urban environment where most of us have to live can be a bit hard to take.

Writing can affect us in the same way, so I would recommend that when you do any of the exercises in this book you build in some space – some 'space around the space' – to absorb the effects properly. When so much of life is a race against the clock, let writing be a place where we can slow everything down: a time for absorption and reconciliation of our divided and different selves. And also a place to take risks: perhaps the biggest risk we can take is to stop being so frantic and start becoming more focused.

However, my overriding memory of leaving that first retreat was somewhat different to what I had been warned to expect. I walked away from the retreat with Dhammarati, the man who had first taught me to meditate at the London Buddhist Centre a few weeks earlier. Dhammarati is a no-nonsense Glaswegian with a lively and alert interest in the world around him, particularly its political and cultural currents. If previously my idea of Buddhists had been of slightly unworldly people seeking to withdraw from society, no one could have contradicted it more than Dhammarati.

As we walked to the railway station he remarked that although it was sound advice to be a little cautious on leaving a retreat, in many ways he took the reverse view. 'After I have been meditating I always think the world should look out for me because I feel so much more robust and potent.' I immediately liked this idea because it turns the spiritual life into something empowering. It means we are gazing into the future, towards our goal, as much as looking back at the things from which we are trying to distance ourselves. It is planting a seed, recognizing that there are all sorts of capacities within us of which we are only dimly aware.

Dhammarati's words were still ringing in my ears a few years later when I became a fund-raiser for a Buddhist charity, the Karuna Trust, which works among some of the poorest communities in India. This work entailed knocking on people's doors and asking if they would like to make a regular financial contribution. As you can imagine, this is a rather daunting prospect, and even though I have now been involved with fund-raising for nearly twenty years, it is no less challenging. I must continually remind myself that each door is different. There can be no 'script' or handbook of responses, because one can never predict what is going to happen. The only strategy is to try to become comfortable being in the unknown, standing, if you like, in that gap between the wolf and the door.

Generally speaking, there are two types of fear that emerge in this gap: the fear of failure and, perhaps more surprisingly, the fear of success. The fear of failure has been a common theme running through these pages. It is the critical voice that says, 'Someone like you will never be a writer,' or indeed a fund-raiser, or anything else for that matter, since the critic's list of things we cannot do is endless. But fear of success? What is that about? If this seems less explicable, it is because it often appears as a wolf in sheep's clothing – though a sheep in wolf's clothing might be more appropriate. It is disguised as something else: good acceptable things like tact (fear of offending others) and modesty (fear of appearing boastful). The trouble is that this is a false modesty that all too easily turns into jealousy and resentment.

No less than fear of failure, fear of success compels us to continue behaving in a certain way, since it has a lot to do with not wanting to appear exceptional and stand out from the crowd. Far from the broad horizons of experimentation where everything is alive with possibility, the fear of success, as with all fears, narrows things down and blocks us in the hope of keeping life safe and predictable. Unfortunately, this condemns us to a limited existence so that we never find out what we are really capable of.

Fear removes us from the present moment; all we can see before us are those things we dread. So I would like to suggest that the next time you pick up a pen to write, start by saying to yourself, 'Maybe I am about to write the best thing I have ever written.' It can do no harm – you can always drop the idea if it becomes a burden – and it might take you somewhere you have never been before. Another threshold, another door. Forget the sheep's clothing, just be the wolf.

Exercise: ## Welcoming Success

Take ten minutes and write about all you could be if you were really successful. Don't be modest; be boastful and outrageous. Write down all the things you have never allowed yourself to say before. Don't worry about punctuation, or grammar, or whether what you write is nonsense or just plain embarrassing; that might be the inner critic trying to trip you up. Just keep writing. Lower your standards, but don't lower your sights.

28

Car Mechanics

Someone recently backed into my car. No one was injured and not much damage was done. Still, my initial relief was followed by what can best be described as dismay – woven through with an underlying panic. 'Oh no,' I kept thinking to myself, 'Yet another thing to be sorted out that will keep me away from writing,' – writing this book as it happens.

This was hardly a useful response. It is true that writers need what Robert Bly has called cunning – rearranging their life in ways that keep them in touch with the inner experiences that cause them to write. Bly compares Walt Whitman, whose cunning was to be surrounded by other human beings – riding Manhattan street cars, crossing on the Brooklyn Ferry, and so on – with Rilke, whose poetry required him to undergo long periods of solitude: a need so deep that he willingly endured years of loneliness.

Cunning, however, is not the same as control-freakery. The first stems from abundance, a sense that our inner world is full of riches that are worth nurturing and protecting. OK, they may be vulnerable to theft, but at least we have faith in their continuing value. But when this becomes an obsessive need to control everything that happens to us, it is a form of impoverishment, if not imprisonment. Not only will we screen out all sorts of interesting encounters that could actually enrich our work, it also suggests that we believe our ideas to be so feeble they will wither and die if we do not immediately capture them. We are snatching at the things we write about when we should be caressing them –

desperation, we might say, highjacking development. As always, it is our motivation that makes the distinction.

William Stafford, for example, worked on his poetry early each morning – a chance to 'let things happen', as he described it – a discipline he maintained for over forty years. Yet when asked how he felt if circumstances prevented him from writing, he replied, 'I forgive myself for those days, it's not a fetish.' Writing was not a fixation or a mania, it was something he simply loved to do. But he could also do without it. You must hold your tricks lightly, as a magician friend once told me. If our motive is more neurotic – writing to seek approval, to try to justify our place on the planet – then too much is at stake. It will be scary to stop doing the one thing that we hope answers our needs. We have begun to confuse writing with life.

In contrast, notice that Stafford is able to say he 'forgives' himself when he cannot find the time for poetry. This is of a piece with his whole philosophy of non-violence, Stafford having been a life-long pacifist. How absurd it would be to try to spread love to the world and not include himself. Yet isn't this what so many of us do? It is a problem of compartmentalization, believing that the ideals that hold in one part of our life can be put to one side when it comes to another.

Our tendency should be towards wholeness. We must keep bringing the wolf to the door, which means that in our writing we should seek unification with, not denial of, the life (our life) that supports it. Sangharakshita, the founder of the Western Buddhist Order, uses the example of work: 'Unless your work is your meditation, your meditation is not meditation.' Any good developed in the shrine-room will quickly be undone if our daily actions are not in accord with the kindness and awareness that underlies our meditation, which means we need to make more balanced and creative efforts in everything we do.

Part of the problem is that we tend to view writers from the Hollywood perspective: solitary geniuses, starving in their garrets, misunderstood and pilloried by the society around them, even feeling that something is wrong if creativity comes too easily. This is going to be a dead end for most of us – I say 'most of us' because there is always that matter of 'cunning'. Gary Snyder, who supported his writing and early studies of Zen Buddhism by working as a forestry labourer and a seaman, said that if you want to become a poet, apprentice yourself to a craftsman such as a carpenter or a car mechanic. This is clearly meant to provoke our romantic notions of the artist, but it makes a lot of sense. He is reminding us that teachers and teachings are everywhere, and that what you do is not as important as how you do it. In the same way, although we have no control over where the next accident will come from, we can choose where it will take us.

The mechanics at my local garage – there are only three of them – are geniuses at multi-tasking, improvising in order to save customers' money, and staying focused while constantly being interrupted. (Contrast this with my precarious attitude to writing.) When I took my car round to them, I noticed for the first time, in their tiny little office, where the whole operation is run so efficiently, an oil-stained poster with the following inscription:

> *I've been beaten, choked, kicked, lied to,*
> *swindled, taken advantage of, and laughed at.*
> *The only reason I hang around is*
> *to see what happens next.*

Notes and References

1

Raymond Carver, 'The Hair', in *No Heroics Please*, Harvill, London 1991, p.43.

2

I am grateful to Sophia March for allowing me to quote the list of things she didn't bring to the Wolf at the Door workshop, Rivendell Buddhist Retreat Centre, near Uckfield, East Sussex, March 2003.

3

For a fuller introduction to the metta bhavana, see for example Paramananda, *Change Your Mind*, Windhorse Publications, Birmingham 1996, chapter 3.

4

Samuel Beckett, *Krapp's Last Tape*, Faber, London 1965, p.20.

5

Ananda (Stephen Parr), 'Onset', in *The School of Monsters*, Wolf at the Door Limited Edition #7, Bristol 2001.

6

Robert Bly, *Iron John*, Addison-Wesley, Reading, MA. 1990, p.32.

7

William Stafford, 'Note', in *The Way It Is: New & Selected Poems*, Graywolf Press, Saint Paul, MN. 1998, p.126.

8

I am grateful to Guhyaratna for allowing me to quote his timed writing from the Wolf at the Door workshop at Sudarshanaloka Buddhist Retreat Centre, Thames, New Zealand, in December 2001.

9

Stephen Dunning and William Stafford, *Getting the Knack: Twenty Poetry Writing Exercises*, National Council of Teachers of English, Urbana, IL. 1992.

10

I am grateful to Sharon Thomas for allowing me to quote 'Sunday Morning' written at the Wolf at the Door workshop, Rivendell, near Uckfield, East Sussex, March 2003.

11

Louis MacNeice's, 'Sunday Morning', can be found in *101 Sonnets from Shakespeare to Heaney*, edited by Don Paterson, Faber, London 1999, p.94.

12

Puja: The FWBO Book of Buddhist Devotional Texts, Windhorse Publications, Birmingham 1999, p.21.

13

Philip Larkin, 'The Building', in *High Windows*, Faber, London 1974, p.24.

14

Graham Greene, *The End of the Affair*, Penguin, Harmondsworth 1975, p.19.

15

Paramananda, *Change Your Mind*, Windhorse Publications, Birmingham 1996, chapter 2.

16

James Joyce, *Ulysses*, Penguin, London 2000, p.214.

17

These versions are given in Andrew Lycett, *Ian Fleming*, Weidenfeld & Nicholson, London 1995, p.220.

18

Seamus Heaney '1.I.87', in *Seeing Things*, Faber, London 1991, p.20.

19

I am grateful to Julia Lewis for allowing me to quote her poem 'People Who Come Here', written on a workshop in June 2001.

20

Thomas A. Clark, 'In Praise of Walking', *Distance & Proximity*, Pocketbooks, Edinburgh 2000, pp.15, 18.

21

I am grateful to Valerie Witonska for permission to quote 'Gertie Contemplates Dhanakosa', written on a workshop in June 2004.

22

W.B. Yeats, 'He wishes for the Cloths of Heaven', *Collected Poems*, Gill & Macmillan, Dublin 1984, p.73.

Sources Consulted

Margaret Atwood, *Negotiating with the Dead: A Writer on Writing*, Cambridge University Press, Cambridge 2002.

Robin Behn & Chase Twichell (eds.), *The Practice of Poetry: Writing Exercises from Poets Who Teach*, HarperPerennial, New York 1992.

Pema Chödrön, *When Things Fall Apart*, Element, London 2003.

E.M. Forster, *Aspects of the Novel*, Pelican, Harmondsworth 1968.

Natalie Goldberg, *Writing Down the Bones: Freeing the Writer Within*, Shambhala, Boston 1986.

Natalie Goldberg, *Wild Mind: Living the Writer's Life*, Shambhala, Boston 1991.

Robert Hass, *The Essential Haiku: Versions of Basho, Buson, & Issa*, Ecco, Hopewell 1994.

Kulananda, *Western Buddhism*, Thorsons, London 1987.

Denise Levertov, *Light Up the Cave*, New Directions, New York 1981.

Paramananda, *Change Your Mind: A Practical Guide to Buddhist Meditation*, Windhorse Publications, Birmingham 1997.

Paramananda, *A Deeper Beauty: Buddhist Reflections on Everyday Life*, Windhorse Publications, Birmingham 2001.

Allison Price, *Writing from the Source: Techniques for Re-Scripting Your Life*, Thorsons, London 1999.

Peter Redgrove, *The Black Goddess and the Sixth Sense*, Paladin, London 1987.

Sangharakshita, *The Ten Pillars Of Buddhism*, Windhorse Publications, Glasgow 1984.

Writing Your Way

Gary Snyder, *The Real Work*, New Directions, New York 1980.

William Stafford, *You Must Revise Your Life*, University of Michigan Press, Ann Arbor, MI, 1986.

William Stafford, *Writing the Australian Crawl: Views on the Writer's Life*, University of Michigan Press, Ann Arbor, MI, 1978.

Wolf at the Door Workshops

For more information about Wolf at the Door writing workshops please visit
www.wolfatthedoor.org
or write to Manjusvara
c/o Windhorse Publications
169 Mill Road
Cambridge
CB1 3AN
UK

Index

Index

About Windhorse Publications

Windhorse Publications is a Buddhist publishing house, staffed by practising Buddhists. We place great emphasis on producing books of high quality, accessible and relevant to those interested in Buddhism at whatever level. Drawing on the whole range of the Buddhist tradition, our books include translations of traditional texts, commentaries, books that make links with Western culture and ways of life, biographies of Buddhists, and works on meditation.

As a charitable institution we welcome donations to help us continue our work. We also welcome manuscripts on aspects of Buddhism or meditation. To join our email list, place an order, or request a catalogue please visit our website at www.windhorsepublications.com or contact:

Windhorse Publications Ltd.   Perseus Distribution   Windhorse Books
169 Mill Road   1094 Flex Drive   P O Box 574
Cambridge CB1 3AN   Jackson TN 38301   Newtown NSW 2042
UK   USA   Australia

About the FWBO

Windhorse Publications is an arm of the Friends of the Western Buddhist Order, which has more than sixty centres worldwide. It runs several successful businesses and the Karuna Trust, a fundraising charity that supports social welfare projects in the slums and villages of Southern Asia.

For more information about the FWBO please visit the website at www.fwbo.org or write to:

London Buddhist Centre   Aryaloka   Sydney Buddhist Centre
51 Roman Road   14 Heartwood Circle   24 Enmore Road
London E2 0HU   Newmarket NH 03857   Sydney NSW 2042
UK   USA   Australia

By the same author

The Poet's Way

In this accessible guide, Manjusvara tackles the essential elements of poetry writing. With imaginative and inspiring exercises, he illuminates the craft, providing a practical guide to writing and sharpening up your own work.

With Buddhist reflections on the writing process and considering issues such as influence, memory and the relationship with prayer and ritual he encourages the engagement of your own life in your writing and the unleashing of your creativity - showing how poetry can reveal new aspects of your spiritual life.

ISBN 9781 907314 04 9
£8.99 / $12.95 / €12.95
160 pages